The *S*
the *Gold*

The Secret of the Golden Flower

The Classic Chinese Book of Life

Translated, with Introduction, Notes, and Commentary by

Thomas Cleary

HarperOne
An Imprint of HarperCollinsPublishers

HarperOne

HarperCollins books may be purchased for educational, business, or sales promotional use. For information, please e-mail the Special Markets Department at SPsales@harpercollins.com.

HarperCollins Web site: http://www.harpercollins.com

HarperCollins®, 📖®, and HarperOne™ are trademarks of HarperCollins Publishers.

Library of Congress Cataloging-in-Publication Data
Lü, Tung-pin, b. 798
   [T'ai i chin hua tsung chih. English]
   The secret of the golden flower / translated, with introduction, notes, and commentary, by Thomas Cleary. — 1st ed.
      p. cm.
   Translation of: T'ai i chin hua tsung chih.
   ISBN: 978–0–06–250193–6
   1. Spiritual life (Taoism) 2. Spiritual life (Buddhism)
I. Cleary, Thomas F., 1949–   II. Title.
BL1923.L78   1991
299'.5144—dc20   90–55796

23 24 25 26 27 LBC 51 50 49 48 47

Contents

Introduction

Naturalness is called the Way.
The Way has no name or form;
it is just the essence,
just the primal spirit.

The Secret of the Golden Flower is a lay manual of Buddhist and Taoist methods for clarifying the mind. A distillation of the inner psychoactive elements in ancient spiritual classics, it describes a natural way to mental freedom practiced in China for many centuries.

The golden flower symbolizes the quintessence of the paths of Buddhism and Taoism. Gold stands for light, the light of the mind itself; the flower represents the blossoming, or opening up, of the light of the mind. Thus the expression is emblematic of the basic awakening of the real self and its hidden potential.

In Taoist terms, the first goal of the Way is to restore the original God-given spirit and become a self-realized human being. In Buddhist terms, a realized human being is someone conscious of the original mind, or the real self, as it is in its spontaneous natural state, independent of environmental conditioning.

This original spirit is also called the celestial mind, or the natural mind. A mode of awareness subtler and more direct than thought or imagination, it is central to the

1

blossoming of the mind. *The Secret of the Golden Flower* is devoted to the recovery and refinement of the original spirit.

This manual contains a number of helpful meditation techniques, but its central method is deeper than a form of meditation. Using neither idea nor image, it is a process of getting right to the root source of awareness itself. The aim of this exercise is to free the mind from arbitrary and unnecessary limitations imposed upon it by habitual fixation on its own contents. With this liberation, Taoists say, the conscious individual becomes a "partner of creation" rather than a prisoner of creation.

The experience of the blossoming of the golden flower is likened to light in the sky, a sky of awareness vaster than images, thoughts, and feelings, an unimpeded space containing everything without being filled. Thus it opens up an avenue to an endless source of intuition, creativity, and inspiration. Once this power of mental awakening has been developed, it can be renewed and deepened without limit.

The essential practice of the golden flower requires no apparatus, no philosophical or religious dogma, no special paraphernalia or ritual. It is practiced in the course of daily life. It is near at hand, being in the mind itself, yet it involves no imagery or thought. It is remote only in the sense that it is a use of attention generally unfamiliar to the mind habituated to imagination and thinking.

The Secret of the Golden Flower is remarkable for the sharpness of its focus on a very direct method for self-realization accessible to ordinary lay people. When it was written down in a crisis more than two hundred years ago, it was a concentrated revival of an ancient teaching; and it has been periodically revived in crises since, due to the rapidity with which the method can awaken awareness of hidden resources in the mind.

The Secret of the Golden Flower is the first book of its kind to have been translated into a Western language. A German version by Richard Wilhelm was first published in 1929, and an English translation of this German rendition was published shortly thereafter. Both German and English editions included an extensive commentary by the distinguished psychologist C. G. Jung, whose work became a major influence in Western psychology, studies of mythology and religion, and New Age culture in general.

Although Jung credited *The Secret of the Golden Flower* with having clarified his own work on the unconscious, he maintained serious reservations about the practice taught in the book. What Jung did not know was that the text he was reading was in fact a garbled translation of a truncated version of a corrupted recension of the original work.

Unawares, a critical communication gap occurred in the process of transmission; and yet the book made a powerful impression. It became one of the main sources of Western knowledge of Eastern spirituality and also one of the seminal influences in Jungian thought on the psychology of religion. Cary F. Baynes, who rendered Wilhelm's German into English, even went so far as to hail it as "the secret of the power of growth latent in the psyche."

Psychological and experiential approaches to religion have enriched modern psychological thought and research, which have in turn enriched the understanding and experience of religion. In terms of religion as culture, one of the advantages of a psychological approach is the facility with which emotional boundaries of church and sect can thereby be transcended.

In Wilhelm's own introduction to his translation of *The Secret of the Golden Flower,* he notes that Taoist organizations following this teaching in his time included not only Confucians and Buddhists but also Jews, Christians, and Muslims, all without requiring them to break away from their own religious congregations. So fundamental is the golden flower awakening that it brings out inner dimensions in all religions.

From the point of view of that central experience, it makes no more difference whether one calls the golden flower awakening a relationship to God or to the Way, or whether one calls it the holy spirit or the Buddha nature or the real self. The *Tao Te Ching* says, "Names can be designated, but they are not fixed terms."

The image of the opening up of the golden flower of the light in the mind is used as but one of many ways of alluding to an effect that is really ineffable. The pragmatic purpose of Taoist and Buddhist teachings is to elicit experience, not to inculcate doctrines; that is why people of other religions, or with no religion at all, have been able to avail themselves of the psychoactive technologies of Taoism and Buddhism without destroying their own cultural identities.

Considered in terms of its essential aim rather than the forms it can take, the golden flower method can be used to transcend the barriers of personal and cultural differences without losing the richness of diversity and distinction.

The Secret of the Golden Flower is indeed a powerful treatise on awakening the hidden potential of a universal human being, and it is in reality an even better and more useful book than Wilhelm, Jung, or Baynes thought it to be. However immature his rendition may have been, I am deeply indebted to Richard Wilhelm for introducing this extraordinary text to the West, for it could otherwise have gone unnoticed for decades, even centuries, amidst the hundreds upon hundreds of Taoist and Buddhist treatises awaiting translation.

It can therefore be said that it is because of Wilhelm's efforts that this new English version of *The Secret of the Golden Flower* has come into being. It is to further inquiries into ways of approaching universal psychology and mental wholeness in general, and to further inquiries into development of the researches initiated by Wilhelm and Jung in their presentation of this book in particular, that I have undertaken to follow up on their work with a new and complete rendition of *The Secret of the Golden Flower*.

Because the still-current Wilhelm/Jung/Baynes edition of this manual contains dangerous and misleading contaminations, a primary consideration of the new translation was to make the contents of *The Secret of the Golden Flower* explicitly accessible to both lay and specialist audiences. This is partly a matter of translation and partly a matter of presentation.

The text itself is somewhat like a series of explanations of practical meanings in esoteric terminology for the use of lay people. To this have been added selections translated from a canonical Chinese Taoist commentary that further refines the principles into pragmatic observations divested of the outward forms of religious and alchemical symbolism. The translation notes explain the expressions, ideas, and practices to which the text refers. The afterword joins the beginning and the end, from the background of the translations to the psychological implications of the praxis.

The Secret of
the Golden Flower

I

The Celestial Mind

1   Naturalness is called the Way. The Way has no name or form; it is just the essence, just the primal spirit.

2   Essence and life are invisible, so they are associated with sky and light. Sky and light are invisible, so they are associated with the two eyes.

3   Since ancient times, those who realized spiritual immortality all communicated their teaching verbally, transmitting it from individual to individual.

4   Taishang appeared magically to Donghua, and the Way was handed on through a succession to Yan, then to the southern and northern schools of Complete Reality, which can be considered its full flourishing.

5   That movement flourished in the sense that there were a great many who followed it, yet it declined in the sense that its mental communication deteriorated. This has continued up to the present day, when it is extremely confused and extremely degenerate.

6 When an extreme is reached, there is a reversion. Therefore there was a certain master Siu who extended his kindness to liberate all, especially setting up the teaching of the special transmission outside of doctrine. For those who heard, it was a rare opportunity; those who accepted it formed a religious association in their time. Everyone should respectfully understand the heart of master Siu.

7 First establish a firm foothold in daily activities within society. Only then can you cultivate reality and understand essence.

8 In obedience to a directive, I am acting as a guide to liberation. Now I am bringing to light the source message of the golden flower of absolute unity. After that I will explain in detail.

9 The absolute unity refers to what cannot be surpassed. There are very many alchemical teachings, but all of them make temporary use of effort to arrive at effortlessness; they are not teachings of total transcendence and direct penetration. The doctrine I transmit directly brings up working with essence and does not fall into a secondary method. That is the best thing about it.

10 The golden flower is light. What color is light? It is symbolized by the golden flower, which [in Chinese characters] also conceals [the words] *one light* within. This is the absolutely unified real energy of celestial immortals; this is what is meant by the saying, "The lead in the homeland of water is just one flavor."

11 The whole work of turning the light around uses the method of reversal. The beauties of the highest heavens and the marvels of the sublimest realms are all within the heart: this is where the perfectly open and aware spirit concentrates. Confucians call it the open center, Buddhists call it the pedestal of awareness, Taoists call it the ancestral earth, the yellow court, the mysterious pass, the primal opening.

12 The celestial mind is like a house; the light is the master of the house. Therefore once you turn the light around, the energies throughout the body all rise. Just turn the light around; this is the unexcelled sublime truth.

13 The light is easily stirred and hard to stabilize. When you have turned it around for a long time, the light crystallizes. This is the natural spiritual body, and it steadies the spirit above the nine skies. This is what is referred to in the *Mind Seal Scripture* as "silently paying court" and "soaring upward."

14 The golden flower is the same thing as the gold pill. The transmutations of spiritual illumination are all guided by mind.

II

The Original Spirit and the Conscious Spirit

1   From the point of view of the universe, people are like mayflies; but from the point of view of the Way, even the universe is as an evanescent reflection. Only the true essence of the original spirit transcends the primal organization and is above it.

2   Vitality and energy degenerate along with the universe, but the original spirit is still there; this is the infinite. The production of the universe all derives from this. If learners can just preserve the original spirit, they live transcendentally outside of yin and yang. They are not within the three realms.

3   This is possible only by seeing essence. This is what is called the original face.

4   What is most wondrous is when the light has crystallized in a spiritual body, gradually becoming consciously effective, and is on the verge of moving into action. This is the secret that has not been transmitted in a thousand ages.

5   The conscious mind is like a violent general of a
    strong fiefdom controlling things from a distance,
    until the sword is turned around.

6   Now steadily keep to the chamber of the origin,
    turning the light around to look back, and this is like
    having a heroic leader on top with great ministers
    helping. Once the inner government is orderly, the
    strong and violent naturally become tame.

7   The highest secrets of alchemy are the water of
    vitality, the fire of spirit, and the earth of attention.

8   The water of vitality is the energy of the primal real
    unity. The fire of spirit is illumination. The earth of
    attention is the chamber of the center, the celestial
    mind.

9   The fire of spirit is the function, the earth of atten-
    tion is the substance, the water of vitality is the
    foundation.

10 People create the body by attention. The body is not
    just the physical body, because there is a lower soul
    therein. The lower soul functions in association with
    consciousness, and consciousness develops based on
    the lower soul. The lower soul is dim; it is the sub-
    stance of consciousness. If consciousness is not inter-
    rupted, transformation and transmutation of the
    lower soul go on endlessly from lifetime to lifetime,
    generation to generation.

11   Then there is the higher soul, which is where the spirit is concealed. The higher soul resides in the eyes during the day and lodges in the liver at night. When it resides in the eyes, it sees; when it lodges in the liver, it dreams.

12   Dreams are the roaming of the spirit. It traverses the nine heavens and nine earths in an instant. If you are dull and depressed on awakening, that is a sign of clinging to the body, which means clinging to the lower soul.

13   So turning the light around is a means of refining the higher soul, which is a means of preserving the spirit, which is a means of controlling the lower soul, which is a means of interrupting consciousness.

14   The ancients' method of transcending the world, refining away the dregs of darkness to restore pure light, is just a matter of dissolving the lower soul and making the higher soul whole.

15   Turning the light around is the secret of dissolving darkness and controlling the lower soul. There is no exercise to restore *the creative,* only the secret of turning the light around. The light itself is *the creative;* to turn it around is to restore it.

16   Just persist in this method, and naturally the water of vitality will be full, the fire of spirit will ignite, the earth of attention will stabilize, and thus the embryo of sagehood can be solidified.

17 A dung beetle rolls a pill of dung, from which life
    emerges, by the pure effort of concentration of spirit.
    If life can come even from a dung ball, how could it
    not be possible to produce a body by concentrating
    the spirit on where the celestial mind rests when the
    embryo leaves the shell?

18 Once the true nature of unified awareness has fallen
    into the chamber of *the creative*, it divides into higher
    and lower souls. The higher soul is in the celestial
    mind; this is yang, energy that is light and clear. This
    is obtained from cosmic space and has the same form
    as the original beginning. The lower soul is yin,
    energy that is dense and opaque. This sticks to the
    ordinary mind that has form.

19 The higher soul likes life, the lower soul looks toward
    death. All lust affecting the temperament is the doing
    of the lower soul. This is what consciousness is. After
    death it feeds on blood, in life it suffers greatly. This
    is darkness returning to darkness, by a coming
    together of kind.

20 If learners refine the dark lower soul completely, then
    it will be pure light.

III

Turning the Light Around and Keeping to the Center

1 Where did the term *turning the light around* begin? It began with the adept Wenshi. When the light is turned around, the energies of heaven and earth, yin and yang, all congeal. This is what is called "refined thought," "pure energy," or "pure thought."

2 When you first put this technique into practice, there is seemingly nonbeing within being. Eventually, when the work is accomplished, and there is a body beyond your body, there is seemingly being within nonbeing.

3 Only after a hundred days of concentrated work is the light real; only then is it the fire of spirit. After a hundred days, the light is spontaneous: a point of true positive energy suddenly produces a pearl, just as an embryo forms from the intercourse of a man and a woman. Then you should attend it calmly and quietly. The turning around of the light is the "firing process."

4   In the original creation there is positive light, which
     is the ruling director. In the material world it is the
     sun; in human beings it is the eyes. Nothing is worse
     than to have a running leakage of spirit and con-
     sciousness; this is conformity, so the way of the
     golden flower is accomplished completely through
     the method of reversal.

5   Turning the light around is not turning around the
     light of one body, but turning around the very
     energy of Creation. It is not stopping random imagi-
     nation only temporarily; it is truly emptying routine
     compulsion for all time.

6   Therefore each breath corresponds to one year of
     human time; and each breath corresponds to a cen-
     tury in the various pathways of the long night of
     ignorance.

7   Usually people wind up pursuing objects and come
     to age in conformity with life, never once looking
     back. When their positive energy fades and disap-
     pears, this is the netherworld. Therefore the *Heroic
     March Scripture* says, "Pure thought is flight, pure
     emotion is fall." When students have little thought
     and much emotion, they sink into low ways. Just
     observe clearly, and when your breath grows quiet
     you then become accurately aware. This is application
     of the method of reversal.

8   This is what is meant in the *Yin Convergence Classic* when it says, "The mechanism is in the eyes," and the *Plain Questions of the Yellow Emperor* when it says, "The light rays of the human body all flow upward into the aperture of space." If you get this, long life is herein, and so is transcendence of life.

9   This is a practice that pervades the three teachings.

10   The light is neither inside nor outside the self. Mountains, rivers, sun, moon, and the whole earth are all this light, so it is not only in the self. All the operations of intelligence, knowledge, and wisdom are also this light, so it is not outside the self. The light of heaven and earth fills the universe; the light of one individual also naturally extends through the heavens and covers the earth. Therefore once you turn the light around, everything in the world is turned around.

11   The light rays are concentrated upward into the eyes; this is the great key of the human body. You should reflect on this. If you do not sit quietly each day, this light flows and whirls, stopping who knows where. If you can sit quietly for a while, all time—ten thousand ages, a thousand lifetimes—is penetrated from this. All phenomena revert to stillness. Truly inconceivable is this sublime truth.

12 Nevertheless, the actual practice goes from shallow to deep, from crude to fine. Throughout, it is best to be consistent. The practice is one from beginning to end, but its quality during the process can be known only by oneself. Nevertheless, it is necessary to wind up at the point where "heaven is open, earth is broad, and all things are just as they are," for only this can be considered attainment.

13 What has been communicated through successive sages is not beyond reversed gazing. Confucians call it "reaching toward knowledge." Buddhists call it "observing mind." Taoists call it "inner observation."

14 The essential teaching is summarized above; as for the rest, matters of entering and exiting stillness, the prelude and the aftermath, one should use the book *Small Stopping and Seeing* for a touchstone.

15 The words *focus on the center* are most sublime. The center is omnipresent; the whole universe is within it. This indicates the mechanism of Creation; you focus on this to enter the gate, that is all. To focus means to focus on this as a hint, not to become rigidly fixated. The meaning of the word *focus* has life to it; it is very subtle.

16 The terms *stopping* and *seeing* basically cannot be sepa-
    rated. They mean concentration and insight. Here-
    after, whenever thoughts arise, you don't need to sit
    still as before, but you should investigate this
    thought: where is it? Where does it come from?
    Where does it disappear? Push this inquiry on and on
    over and over until you realize it cannot be grasped;
    then you will see where the thought arises. You don't
    need to seek out the point of arising any more.
    "'Having looked for my mind, I realize it cannot be
    grasped.' 'I have pacified your mind for you.'"

17 This is correct seeing; whatever is contrary to this is
    false seeing. Once you reach this ungraspability, then
    as before you continuously practice stopping and
    continue it by seeing, practice seeing and continue it
    by stopping. This is twin cultivation of stopping and
    seeing. This is turning the light around.

18 The turning around is stopping, the light is seeing.
    Stopping without seeing is called turning around
    without light; seeing without stopping is called hav-
    ing light without turning it around. Remember this.

IV

Turning the Light Around and Tuning the Breathing

1   The doctrine just requires single-minded practice. One does not seek experiential proof, but experiential proof comes of itself.

2   On the whole, beginners suffer from two kinds of problems: oblivion and distraction. There is a device to get rid of them, which is simply to rest the mind on the breath.

3   The breath is one's own mind; one's own mind does the breathing. Once mind stirs, then there is energy. Energy is basically an emanation of mind.

4   Our thoughts are very rapid; a single random thought takes place in a moment, whereupon an exhalation and inhalation respond to it. Therefore inward breathing and outward breathing accompany each other like sound and echo. In a single day one breathes countless times, so has countless random thoughts. When the luminosity of spirit has leaked out completely, one is like a withered tree or dead ashes.

5   So should one have no thoughts? It is impossible to have no thoughts. Should one not breathe? It is impossible not to breathe. Nothing compares to making the affliction itself into medicine, which means to have mind and breath rest on each other. Therefore tuning the breath should be included in turning the light around.

6   This method makes use of two lights. One is the light of the ears, one is the light of the eyes. The light of the eyes means the external sun and moon, combining their lights; the light of the ears means the internal sun and moon, combining their vitalities. However, vitality is congealed and stabilized light; "they have the same source but different names." Therefore clarity of hearing and seeing are both one and the same spiritual light.

7   When you sit, lower your eyelids and then establish a point of reference. Now let go. But if you let go absolutely, you may not be able to simultaneously keep your mind on listening to your breathing.

8   You should not allow your breathing to actually be audible; just listen to its soundlessness. Once there is sound, you are buoyed by the coarse and do not enter the fine. Then be patient and lighten up a little. The more you let go, the greater the subtlety; and the greater the subtlety, the deeper the quietude.

9   Eventually, after a long time, all of a sudden even the subtle will be interrupted and the true breathing will appear, whereupon the substance of mind will become perceptible.

10   This is because when mind is subtle, breath is subtle; when mind is unified, it moves energy. When breath is subtle, mind is subtle; when energy is unified, it moves mind. Stabilization of mind must be preceded by development of energy because the mind has no place to set to work on; so focus on energy is used as a starting point. This is what is called the preservation of pure energy.

11   You don't understand the meaning of the word *movement*. Movement is pulling the strings; the word *movement* is another word for *control*. Since you can cause movement by vigorous action, how could you not be able to cause stillness by pure quietude?

12   The great sages saw the interrelation of mind and energy and skillfully set up an expedient for the benefit of people of later times. An alchemical text says, "The hen embraces the egg, always mentally listening." These are the finest instructions. The way a hen can give life to an egg is through warm energy; warm energy can only warm the shell and cannot penetrate the inside, so she mentally conducts the energy inward. That "listening" is single-minded concentration. When the mind enters, the energy enters; with warm energy, the birth takes place.

13 Therefore even though the mother hen goes out from time to time, she is always listening, and the concentration of her spirit is never interrupted. Since the concentration of the spirit is never interrupted, then the warm energy is also uninterrupted day and night, so the spirit comes alive.

14 The life of the spirit comes from the prior death of the mind. If people can kill the mind, the original comes alive. Killing the mind does not mean quietism, it means undivided concentration. Buddha said, "Place the mind on one point, and everything can be done."

15 If the mind tends to run off, then unify it by means of the breath; if the breath tends to become rough, then use the mind to make it fine. If you do this, how can the mind fail to stabilize?

16 Generally speaking, the two afflictions of oblivion and distraction just require quieting practice to continue unbroken day after day until complete cessation and rest occur spontaneously. When you are not sitting quietly, you may be distracted without knowing it; but once you are aware of it, distraction itself becomes a mechanism for getting rid of distraction.

17 As for unawares oblivion and oblivion of which you become aware, there is an inconceivable distance between them. Unawares oblivion is real oblivion; oblivion that you notice is not completely oblivious. Clear light is in this.

18 Distraction means the spirit is racing; oblivion means the spirit is unclear. Distraction is easy to cure; oblivion is hard to heal. Using the metaphor of illness, one that involves pain or itch can be treated with medicine, but oblivion is a symptom of paralysis, where there is no feeling.

19 A distracted mind can be concentrated, and a confused mind can be set in order; but oblivion is unformed darkness, in contrast to distraction, which still has some direction.

20 Oblivion means the lower soul is in complete control, whereas the lower soul is a lingering presence in distraction. Oblivion is ruled by pure darkness and negativity.

21 When you are sitting quietly, if you become drowsy, this is oblivion. Repelling oblivion is simply a matter of tuning the breath. The "breath" in this case is respiration, not the "true breathing." Nevertheless the true breathing is present within it.

22 Whenever you sit, you should quiet your mind and unify your energy. How is the mind quieted? The mechanism is in the breathing, but the mind alone knows you are breathing out and in; do not let the ears hear. When you don't hear it, the breathing is fine; and when breathing is fine, the mind is clear. If you can hear it, the breathing is rough, which means the mind is cloudy. Cloudiness means oblivion, so it is natural to feel sleepy. Even so, the mind should be kept on the breathing.

23 It is also essential to understand that this device is not mechanical or forced. Just maintain a subtle looking and listening.

24 What is "looking"? It is the light of the eyes spontaneously shining, the eyes only looking inward and not outward. Not looking outward yet being alert is inward looking; it is not that there really is such a thing as looking inward.

25 What is "listening"? It is the light of the ears spontaneously listening, the ears only listening inward and not outward. Not listening outward yet being alert is inward listening; it is not that there really is such a thing as listening inward.

26 Listening means listening to the soundless; looking means looking at the formless.

27 When the eyes do not look outside and the ears do not listen outside, they are closed in and have a tendency to race around inside. Only by inward looking and listening can you prevent this inner racing as well as oblivion in between. This is the meaning of sun and moon combining their vitalities and lights.

28   When you sink into oblivion and become drowsy, get up and take a walk. When your spirit has cleared, sit again. It's best to sit for a while in the early morning when you have free time. After noontime, when there are many things to do, it's easy to fall into oblivion. Also, there's no need to fix the length of time of meditation; it is only essential to set aside all involvements and sit quietly for a while. Eventually you will attain absorption and not become oblivious or sleepy.

V

Errors in Turning the Light Around

1   Even though your practice gradually matures, "there are many pitfalls in front of the cliff of withered trees." This makes it necessary to elucidate the experiences involved in detail. Only when you have personally gotten this far do you know how I can talk of it now.

2   Our school is not the same as Chan study in that we have step-by-step evidences of efficacy. Let us first talk about points of distinction, then about evidences of efficacy.

3   When you are going to practice this doctrine, first see to it somehow that you don't have much on your mind, so that you can be alive and free. Make your mood gentle and your mind comfortable, then enter into quietude.

4   When you are quiet, it is then essential to find potential and find its opening; don't sit inside nothingness or indifference (so-called "neutral voidness").

5   Even as you let go of all objects, you are alert and self-possessed.

6   But don't get enthusiastic about attaining the experience. (This easily happens whenever reality is taken too seriously. That means not that you shouldn't recognize reality, but that the rhythm of reality is on the brink of existence and nonexistence. You can get it by intent that is not willful.)

7   Even in the midst of alert awareness, you are relaxed and natural. But don't fall into the elements of body and mind, where material and psychological illusions take charge. If you tend to fall into a deadness whenever you go into meditation and are relatively lacking in growth and creative energy, this means you have fallen into a shadow world. Your mood is cold, your breath sinking, and you have a number of other chilling and withering experiences. If you continue this way for a long time, you will degenerate into a blockhead or a rockhead.

8   And yet it will not do to go along with all conditions.

9   Once you have gone into quietude and all sorts of loose ends come to you for no apparent reason, you find you cannot turn them away if you want to, and you even feel comfortable going along with them. This is called the master becoming the servant. If this goes on long, you fall into the various roads of the realms of form and desire.

10   Once you know this, you can seek experiential proofs.

VI

Authenticating Experiences of Turning the Light Around

1   There are many authenticating experiences that cannot be undergone responsibly by people with small faculties and small capacities. You must will the liberation of all beings; you cannot handle attainment with a careless or arrogant attitude.

2   When there is uninterrupted continuity in quiet, the spirit and feelings are joyful and happy, as if one were intoxicated, or in a bath. This is called positive harmony pervading the body, its golden efflorescence suddenly blooming.

3   Once "myriad pipes are all silent," and "the bright moon is in mid sky," you feel the whole earth as a realm of light. This is the opening up of the luminosity that is the substance of mind, the proper release of the golden flower.

4   Once the whole body is filled completely, you do not fear wind or frost. When you meet things that make people feel desolate in facing them, your vital spirit shines even brighter. The house is built of yellow gold, the terrace is white jade; the rotten things of the world you bring to life with a puff of true energy. Red blood becomes milk, the physical body is all gold and jewels. This is the great stabilization of the golden flower.

5   The first stage corresponds to the *Visualization Scripture*'s technical symbols of the setting sun, the great body of water, and the trees in rows. The setting of the sun stands for setting up the foundation in the undifferentiated; this is the infinite. "Higher good is like water," flawlessly pure; this is the ultimate. The master is the ruler that produces movement, and since movement is symbolized by wood, it is repre-sented by trees in rows. The rows are in sevens, which stand for the light of the seven openings of the "heart."

6   The second stage begins from the foundation; at this point the whole earth becomes a jewel ground of ice crystals; the light gradually solidifies. Therefore a great terrace follows. As for the Buddha on the ter-race of enlightenment, once the golden essence has become manifest, what is it if not Buddha? Buddha is the "gold immortal" of great awareness. This is just the authenticating experience of the major stage.

7   There are three authenticating experiences that can
    be considered now. One is when you are sitting and
    the spirit enters into a state of openness, and then
    when you hear people talking it is as though from far
    away, but everything is clearly understood even
    though all sounds coming in are like echoes in a
    valley. All are heard, you have never heard anything
    yourself. This is the spirit in a state of openness; it
    can be experienced by oneself at any time.

8   Another experience is when in the midst of quiet the
    light of the eyes blazes up, filling one's presence with
    light. It is like opening the eyes in a cloud. There is
    no way to look for one's body. This is "the empty
    room producing light." Inside and outside are per-
    meated with light, auspicious signs hover in stillness.

9   Yet another experience is when in the midst of quiet
    the energy of the physical body becomes like silk or
    jade; while sitting, if you don't stop it, the energy
    will soar buoyantly upward. This is the spirit return-
    ing to the highest heaven. Eventually, after a long
    time, it is thereby possible to ascend.

10 These three experiences can be verified now, but it is
    still not possible to explain them thoroughly. People
    experience higher things individually, according to
    their faculties and capacities. This is like what *Stopping
    and Seeing* calls the emerging manifestations of roots
    of good.

11   These things are like when people drink water and know for themselves whether it is cool or warm: it is necessary for you to attain faith on your own. Only then is the true primal unified energy present.

12   If you find the unified energy yourself in authenticating experience, the elixir immediately crystallizes. This is a grain of reality. "A grain, and then another grain, from vagueness to clarity." This refers to the "primal grain" that builds up through time; there is also the total primal grain, which is measureless.

13   Each grain has a grain's power. This requires individual fortitude above all.

VII

The Living Method of Turning the Light Around

1   As you go along practicing turning the light around, you need not give up your normal occupation. An ancient said, "When matters come up, one should respond; when things come up, one should discern."

2   If you manage affairs with accurate mindfulness, then the light is not overcome by things, so it will do to repeat this formless turning around of the light time and again.

3   If you can look back again and again into the source of mind, whatever you are doing, not sticking to any image of person or self at all, then this is "turning the light around wherever you are." This is the finest practice.

4   In the early morning, if you can clear all objects from your mind and sit quietly for one or two hours, that is best. Whenever you are engaged in work or dealing with people, just use this "looking back" technique, and there will be no interruption. If you practice in this way for two or three months, the realized ones in Heaven will surely come to attest to your experience.

VIII

The Secret of Freedom

1 Jadelike purity has left a secret of freedom
In the lower world:
Congeal the spirit in the lair of energy,
And you'll suddenly see
White snow flying in midsummer,
The sun blazing in the water at midnight.
Going along harmoniously,
You roam in the heavens
Then return to absorb
The virtues of *the receptive*.

2 There is another line, a mystery within a mystery:
"The homeland of nothing whatsoever is the true
abode." The depths of the mystery are all contained
in a single measured verse.

3 The essence of the great Way is to act purposefully
without striving. Because of nonstriving, one does
not cling to local conventions, forms, or images; but
because of not striving yet acting purposefully, one
does not fall into indifferent emptiness, dead voidness.

4   The function is all in the center, but the mechanism
     is all in the two eyes. The two eyes are the handle of
     the stars, which manages Creation and operates yin
     and yang.

5   The major medicinal ingredient beginning to end is
     only the "metal in the middle of primary water" (i.e.,
     the "lead in the region of water"). The preceding talk
     of turning the light around points out a method for
     beginners to control the inside from outside, thus
     helping them to attain independence.

6   This is for middling and lesser people cultivating the
     lower two passes in order to penetrate the upper
     pass. Now as the Way gradually becomes clear and
     mastery of the device gradually matures, Heaven does
     not begrudge the Way but directly divulges the
     unsurpassed doctrine. Keep it confidential, and
     work it out.

7   *Turning the light around* is only the general term: with
     each level of progress in practice, the efflorescence of
     the light increases in magnitude, and the method of
     turning around becomes subtler. Previously one con-
     trolled the inside from the outside; now one abides
     in the center and controls the outside. Before, the
     assistant administered for the master; now one
     promulgates policy in service of the master. There has
     manifestly been a great reversal.

8   When you want to enter quietude, first tune and concentrate body and mind, so that they are free and peaceful. Let go of all objects, so that nothing whatsoever hangs on your mind, and the celestial mind takes its rightful place in this center.

9   After that, lower your eyelids and gaze inward at the chamber of *water*. Where the light reaches, true positive energy comes forth in response.

10   *Fire* is yang outside and yin inside, so it is in substance *the creative*, with one yin inside ruling it, arousing mind according to things, going along out into habitual routines.

11   Now when you turn the light around to shine inward, [the mind] is not aroused by things; negative energy then stops, and the flower of light radiates a concentrated glow, which is pure positive energy.

12   Correlates inevitably associate, so the positivity in *water* leaps up, whereupon it is not the positivity in *water* but just the positivity in *the creative* itself responding to the positivity in *the creative*. Once the two things meet, they join inextricably, the living movement of creative energy now coming, now going, now floating, now sinking. In the basic chamber in oneself there is an ungraspable sense of vast space, beyond measure; and the whole body feels wondrously light and buoyant. This is what is called "clouds filling the thousand mountains."

13 Next, the coming and going is traceless, the floating and sinking are indiscernible. The channels are stilled, energy stops: this is true intercourse. This is what is called "the moon steeped in myriad waters."

14 When the celestial mind first stirs in the midst of that utter darkness of the unknown, this is the return of initial positive energy. This is "living midnight." So what transpires at this point should be explained in detail.

15 Ordinarily, once people let their eyes and ears pursue things, they get stirred up, only to stop when things are gone. This activity and rest are all subjects, but the sovereign ruler becomes their slave. This is "always living with ghosts."

16 Now if in all activity and rest you abide in heaven while in the midst of humanity, the sovereign is then the real human being. When it moves, you move with it; the movement is the root of heaven. When it is at rest, you rest with it; the rest is the moon cavern.

17 If the celestial mind keeps still and you miss the right timing in action, then that is an error of weakness. If you act in response to it after the celestial mind has acted, this is an error of staleness.

18 Once the celestial mind stirs, then use pure attention to raise it up to the chamber of *the creative,* with the light of spirit focused on the crown of the head to guide it. This is acting in time.

19 When the celestial mind has risen to the peak of *the creative,* it floats upward of its own accord, then suddenly verges on utter quiescence; immediately use pure attention to conduct it into the yellow court, as the light of the eyes is focused on the spiritual room in the center.

20 Once about to enter utter quiescence, not a single thought is born; when gazing inward, suddenly one forgets the gazing. At that time body and mind are in a state of great freedom, and all objects disappear without a trace. Then you don't even know where the furnace and cauldron in your spiritual room are; you can't even find your own body. This is the time when "heaven enters earth" and all wonders return to the root. This is solidifying the spirit in the lair of energy.

21 When you first practice turning the light around and your mind gets scattered or distracted, so you want to concentrate it, your six senses are not used; this is called "nurturing the root source, adding fuel to continue life."

22 Once concentration is attained, you are naturally buoyant and do not expend any strength; this is called "settling the spirit in the original openness, gathering the primal together."

23 When even shadows and echoes have all disappeared, and one is highly stabilized in profound tranquillity, this is called "hibernating in the lair of energy, all wonders returning to the root."

24 These three stages are in each stage, so there are nine stages in one stage. I will expound upon that later; for now I will speak of three stages in one.

25 During the nurturing and initial quieting, gathering is also nurturing, and hibernating is also nurturing. At the end, nurturing is also hibernating. The stage in between can be figured out by analogy.

26 You do not change places, but places are distinguished therein; this is the formless opening, where all places are one place. You do not change times, but times are distinguished therein; this is time without a period, an interval of a world cycle of the original organization.

27 As long as the mind has not reached supreme quiet, it cannot act. Action caused by momentum is random action, not essential action. Therefore it is said that action influenced by things is human desire, while action uninfluenced by things is the action of Heaven.

28 This does not contrast the action of Heaven to the nature of Heaven. There is a line missing [*sic*]. After this I'll explain the word *desire*.

29 Desire is in considering things to exist, or being possessive toward things. This is thought that is out of place, action with an ulterior motive.

30   When not a single thought arises, then true mindfulness is born; this is pure attention. When the celestial potential is suddenly activated in the midst of silent trance, is this not spontaneous attention? This is what is meant by acting without striving.

31   The first two lines of the verse at the beginning of this chapter wrap up the function of the golden flower. The next two lines refer to the interchange of sun and moon; "midsummer" stands for the "fire" of [the trigrammatic *Book of Change* symbol] *fire*. The "white snow" is the true yin within *fire* about to return to *earth*. "Midnight" is the water of *water*. The "sun" is the single yang in the center of *water* on the verge of blazing and returning to *heaven*. Herein lies [the operation of spiritual alchemy known as] "taking from *water* to fill in *fire*."

32   The next two lines explain the function of the dipper handle, the whole mechanism of rising and descending. Does not "in the water" refer to *water*? The eyes, as the breeze of *wind*, shine into the chamber of *water* and beckon the vitality of dominant yang. That is what these lines mean.

33   "In the heavens" refers to the chamber of *the creative*. "Roaming and returning to absorb the virtues of *the receptive*" means nurturing the fire.

34   The last two lines point out the secret within the secret. The secret within the secret cannot be dispensed with from start to finish. This is what is called cleaning the mind, washing the thoughts, which is "bathing."

35 The learning of sages begins with knowing when to stop and ends with stopping at ultimate good. It begins in the infinite and winds up in the infinite.

36 In Buddhism, activating the mind without dwelling on anything is considered the essential message of the whole canon. In Taoism, "effecting openness" is the whole work of completing essence and life. In sum, the three teachings are not beyond one saying, which is a spiritual pill that gets one out of death and preserves life.

37 What is the spiritual pill? It just means to be unminding in all situations. The greatest secret in Taoism is "bathing." Thus the whole practice described in this book does not go beyond the words "emptiness of mind." It is enough to understand this. This single statement can save decades of seeking.

38 If you do not understand how three stages are included in one, for an analogy let me use the Buddhist teaching of contemplating emptiness, the conditional, and the center.

39 First is emptiness; you see all things as empty. Next is the conditional; though you know things are empty, you do not destroy the totality of things but take a constructive attitude toward all events in the midst of emptiness. Once you neither destroy things nor cling to things, this is the contemplation of the center.

40   When you are practicing the contemplation of emptiness, if you still know that the totality of things cannot be destroyed, and yet do not cling to them, this
includes all three contemplations.

41   Since empowerment after all means really seeing
emptiness, when you cultivate contemplation of
emptiness, emptiness is empty, the conditional is
also empty, and the center is empty too.

42   In practicing contemplation of the conditional, much
of the empowerment is attained in action; so while
the conditional is of course conditional, emptiness is
also conditional and the center is conditional too.

43   When on the way of the center, you still meditate on
emptiness; but you don't call it emptiness, you call it
the center. You also meditate on the conditional; but
you don't call it the conditional, you call it the
center. When you come to the center, there is no
need to say.

44   Although I sometimes speak only of *fire,* sometimes
I also speak of *water.* Ultimately they have never
moved; with one saying I open my mouth: the
essential mechanism is all in the two eyes. The
mechanism means the function; you use this to
manage Creation.

45   This does not mean that is all there is to Creation; all
the faculties of sense and mind are mines of light, so
how could we presume to take only the two eyes and
not deal with the rest?

46   To use the yang of *water*, you use the light of *fire* to illumine and absorb it. This shows that the "sun and moon" are originally one thing.

47   The darkness in the sun is the vitality of the true moon; the "moon cavern" is not on the moon but on the sun. That is why it is called the "moon cavern," for otherwise it would be enough just to say the "moon."

48   The white of the moon is the light of the true sun. The sunlight being on the moon is what is called the "root of heaven." Otherwise it would be enough just to say "heaven."

49   When the sun and moon are separated, they are but half; only when they come together do they form a whole. This is like the case of a single man or a single woman, who cannot form a family living alone; only when there are husband and wife do they amount to a family.

50   But it is hard to represent the Way concretely. If a man and a woman are separated they are still individuals, but if the sun and moon are separated they do not form a complete whole. What I am saying just brings out the point of communion, so I do not see duality; you just cling to the separation, so the separation has taken over your eyes.

IX

Setting Up
the Foundation in a
Hundred Days

1   One of the *Mind Seal* scriptures says, "the returning wind mixes together, the hundred days' work is effective." On the whole, to set up the foundation requires a hundred days before you have real light. As you are, you are still working with the light of the eyes, not the fire of spirit, not the fire of essence, not the torch of wisdom.

2   Turn it around for a hundred days, and the vital energy will naturally be sufficient for true yang to rise spontaneously, so that there is true fire naturally existing in water. If you carry on the practice this way, you will naturally achieve intercourse and formation of the embryo. You are then in the heaven of unknowing, and the child thus develops. If you entertain any conceptual view at all, this is immediately a misleading path.

3   A hundred days setting up the foundation is not a hundred days; one day setting up the foundation is not one day. One breath setting up the foundation does not refer to respiration. Breath is one's own mind; one's own mind is the breath's original spirit, original energy, and original vitality: rising and descending, parting and joining, all arise from mind; being and nonbeing, emptiness and fullness, are all in the thoughts. One breath is held for a lifetime, not only a hundred days; so a hundred days is also a single breath.

4   The hundred days is just a matter of empowerment: gain power in the daytime, and you use it at night; gain power at night, and you use it in the daytime.

5   The hundred days setting up the foundation is a precious teaching. The sayings of the advanced realized ones all relate to the human body; the sayings of true teachers all relate to students. This is the mystery of mysteries, which is inscrutable. When you see essence, you then know why students must seek the direction of a true teacher. Everything that emerges naturally from essence is tested.

X

The Light of Essence and the Light of Consciousness

1 The method of turning the light around basically is to be carried on whether walking, standing, sitting, or reclining. It is only essential that you yourself find the opening of potential.

2 Previously I quoted the saying, "Light arises in the empty room." This light is not luminous, but there is an explanation of this as an evidence of efficacy in the beginning before one has seen the light. If you see it as light and fix your attention on it, then you fall into ideational consciousness, which is not the light of essence.

3 Now when the mind forms a thought, this thought is the present mind. This mind is light; it is medicine. Whenever people look at things, when they perceive them spontaneously all at once without discriminating, this is the light of essence. It is like a mirror reflecting without intending to do so. In a moment it becomes the light of consciousness, through discrimination. When there is an image in a mirror, there is no more mirroring; when there is consciousness in the light, then what light is there any more?

4   At first, when the light of essence turns into thought, then it is consciousness. When consciousness arises, the light is obscured and cannot be found. It is not that there is no light, but that the light has become consciousness. This is what is meant by the saying of the Yellow Emperor, "When sound moves, it does not produce sound, it produces echoes."

5   The introduction to logical examination in the *Heroic March Scripture* says, "neither in objects nor in consciousness," only picking out the organ. What does this mean? Objects are external things, or the so-called material world. This has no actual connection with us. If you pursue objects, you are mistaking things for yourself.

6   Things must have an attribution. Transmission of light is attributable to doors and windows, light is attributable to the sun and moon. Borrowing them for myself, after all I find "it is not mine." When it comes to where "it is not you," then who attributes if not you?

7   "Light is attributable to the sun and moon." When you see the light of the sun and moon, there is nothing to attribute it to. Sometimes there is no sun or moon in the sky, but there is never an absence of the essence of seeing that sees the sun and moon.

8   If so, then can that which discriminates sun and moon be considered one's own possession? Don't you know that discrimination is based on light and dark? When both light and dark are forgotten, then where is discrimination? Therefore there is still attribution; this is an internal object.

9   Only the seeing essence cannot be attributed to anything. But if when seeing seeing, seeing is not seeing, then the seeing essence also has an attribution, which refers back to the seeing essence of the revolving flow of consciousness, alluded to in Buddhist scripture where it says, "Using your flowing revolving consciousness is called error."

10   When first practicing the eight attributions for discerning perception, the first seven show how each is attributable to something, temporarily leaving the seeing essence as a crutch for the practitioner. But ultimately as long as the seeing essence still carries with it the eighth consciousness, it is not really unattributable. Only when this last point is broken through is this the real seeing essence, which is truly unattributable.

11   When turning the light around, you properly turn around the primary unattributable light, so not a single conscious thought is applied.

12   What causes you to flow and revolve is just the six
     sense organs; but what enables you to attain enlight-
     enment is also just the six sense organs. But the fact
     that sense objects and sense consciousnesses are not
     used at all does not mean using the sense organs, just
     using the essence in the sense organs.

13   Now if you turn the light around without falling into
     consciousness, you are using the original essence in
     the sense organs. If you turn the light around fallen
     into consciousness, then you use the nature of con-
     sciousness in the sense organs. Herein lies the hairs-
     breadth's distinction.

14   Deliberate meditation is the light of consciousness;
     let go, and it is then the light of essence. A hairs-
     breadth's difference is as that of a thousand miles,
     so discernment is necessary.

15   If consciousness is not stopped, spirit does not come
     alive; if mind is not emptied, the elixir does not
     crystallize.

16   When mind is clean, that is elixir; when mind is
     empty, that is medicine. When it doesn't stick to
     anything at all, it is said that the mind is clean; when
     it doesn't keep anything in it, it is said that the mind
     is empty. If emptiness is seen as empty, emptiness is
     still not empty. When empty and mindless of
     emptiness, this is called true emptiness.

XI

The Intercourse of *Water* and *Fire*

1 Whenever you leak vital spirit, being stirred and interacting with beings, that is all *fire*. Whenever you gather back spirit's consciousness and quiet it down to steep in the center, that is all *water*. When the senses run outward, that is *fire;* when the senses turn around inward, that is *water.*

2 The one yin [inside the *fire* trigram] concentrates on pursuing sense experience, while the one yang [inside the *water* trigram] concentrates on reversing and withdrawing the senses themselves.

3 Water and fire are yin and yang, yin and yang are essence and life, essence and life are body and mind, body and mind are spirit and energy. Once you withdraw to rest your vital spirit and are not influenced by objects, then this is true intercourse, as of course when you sit in profound silence.

XII

The Cycle

1   For the complete cycle, energy is not the main thing; mental attainment is the sublime secret. If you wonder what it ultimately is, the cycle helps growth; it is maintained without minding, carried out without deliberate intention.

2   Look up at the sky; it changes from hour to hour, through 365 days, yet the polar star never moves. Our mind is also like this; mind is the pole, energy is the myriad stars revolving around it. The energy in our limbs and throughout our whole body is basically a network, so do not exert your strength to the full on it. Refine the conscious spirit, remove arbitrary views, and then after that medicine will develop.

3   This medicine is not a material thing; it is the light of essence, which is none other than the primal true energy. Even so, it is necessary to attain great concentration before you see it. There is no method of culling; those who speak of culling are quite mistaken.

4   When you have seen it for a long time, eventually the light of the basis of the mind becomes spontaneous. When the mind is empty, and all indulgence is ended, you are liberated from the ocean of misery.

5   If it is "dragon and tiger" today, "water and fire" tomorrow, in the end they turn into illusions.

6   There is a cycle in each day, there is a cycle in each hour; where *water* and *fire* interact, this is a cycle. Our interaction is the "revolving of Heaven." As long as you are unable to stop the mind directly, as a consequence there are times of interaction and times of noninteraction.

7   Yet the revolving of Heaven never stops for a moment. If you are actually able to join yin and yang in tranquillity, the whole earth is positive and harmonious; in the right place in your central chamber, all things simultaneously expand to fulfillment. This is the method of "bathing" spoken of in alchemical classics. What is it if not the great cycle?

8   The processes of the cycle do indeed have differences of scale, but ultimately there is no way to distinguish great and small. When you reach the point where meditation is spontaneous, you do not know what *fire* and *water* are, what heaven and earth are, who does the interacting, who makes it one cycle or two cycles, or where to find any distinction between great and small.

9 It is all the operation of one body; though it appears to be most great, it is also small. Each time it takes a turn, the universe and all things take a turn with it. Thus it is in the heart; so it is also most great.

10 The alchemical process should ultimately become spontaneous. If it is not spontaneous, then heaven and earth will revert on their own to heaven and earth; myriad things will go back to myriad things: no matter how hard you try to join them, you cannot. Then it is like a season of drought, when yin and yang do not join. Heaven and earth do not fail to go through their cycles every day, but ultimately you see a lot that is unnatural.

11 If you can operate yin and yang, turning them suitably, then naturally all at once clouds will form and rain will fall, the plants and trees refreshed, the mountain rivers flowing freely. Even if there is something offensive, it still melts away all at once when you notice it. This is the great cycle.

12 Students ask about "living midnight." This is very subtle. If you insist on defining it as true midnight, that would seem to be sticking to forms; but if you do not focus on forms and do not point out true midnight, by what means can the living midnight be known?

13 Once you know living midnight, there is definitely also true midnight. Are they one or two, not true or not alive? It all requires you to see the real. Once you see the real, everything is true, everything is alive. If your seeing is not real, what is living, what is true?

14 As for living midnight, when you see it at all times, finally you reach true midnight; your mood is clear and light, and living midnight gradually blooms into ever-greater awareness.

15 At present, people do not yet clearly know the living; just test it out when you head for the true, and the true will appear, while the living will be sublime.

XIII

Song to Inspire
the World

0 Because of the warmth of my cinnabar heart to liberate the world, I do not refrain from coddling and
talking a lot. Buddha also pointed directly to life and
death for a great cause, and this is truly worthwhile.
Lao-tzu also lamented the existence of the egotistic
self and transmitted the teaching of the open spirit,
but people did not discern. Now I give a general
explanation of finding the road of truth:

1 The pervasive principle of the center
Bears universal change;

2 The very being of true poise
Is the mysterious pass.

3 Midnight, noon, and in between,
If you can stabilize breathing,

4 The light returns to the primal opening,
So all psychic functions are calm.

5 There emerges the unified energy
Of the river source that produces the medicine.

6   It passes through the screen
And transmutes, with golden light;

7   The single disk of the red sun
Shines with constant brilliance.

8   People of the world misconstrue
The vitalities *water* and *fire;*

9   Conveying them from heart and genitals,
Thus producing separation.

10   How can the human way
Meet the celestial mind?

11   If in accord with the celestial,
The way is naturally meet.

12   Put down all objects, so nothing comes to mind;
This is the true infinity of the primal.

13   Cosmic space is silent,
Signs are gone;

14   At the pass of essence and life,
You forget conceptual consciousness.

15   After conceptual consciousness is forgotten,
You see basic reality.

16   The water-clarifying pearl appears,
Mysterious and unfathomable:

17   The screen of beginningless afflictions
Is voided all at once.

18 The jade capital sends down
A team of nine dragons;

19 Walking in the sky,
You climb to the gateway of heaven:

20 Controlling wind and lightning,
You make the thunder rumble.

21 Freezing the spirit and steadying breath are for beginners;
Retreating to hide in secrecy is eternal calm.

22 The two poems I used when I initiated Zhang Zhennu long ago both contain the great Way. "After midnight and before noon" are not times, but *water* and *fire*. "Settling the breath" means a state of centeredness in which you go back to the root with each breath. "Sitting" means that the mind is unmoved. The "mid-spine where the ribs join" does not refer to vertebrae; it is the great road directly through to the jade capital. As for the "double pass," there is something ineffable in this. "Thunder in the earth rumbles, setting in motion rain on the mountain" means the arising of true energy. The "yellow sprouts emerging from the ground" refer to the growth of the medicine.

These two little verses are exhaustive; in them the highway of practical cultivation is clear. These are not confusing words.

Turning the light around is a matter of single-minded practice: just use the true breathing for stable awareness in the central chamber. After a long time at this you will naturally commune with the spirit and attain transmutation.

This is all based on quieting of mind and stabilization of energy. When the mind is forgotten and the energy congeals, this is a sign of effectiveness. The emptiness of energy, breath, and mind is the formation of the elixir. The unification of mind and energy is incubation. Clarifying the mind and seeing its essence is understanding the Way.

You should each practice diligently; it would be too bad if you wasted time. If you do not practice for a day, then you are a ghost for a day; if you do practice for a single breath, then you are a realized immortal for a breath. Work on this.

Questions and Answers Opening up the Mysteries of the Doctrine of the Golden Flower

You suppose that attainment is possible in quietude but lost in activity; you do not realize that the reason for loss through activity is because nothing is attained through stillness. When you attain nothing in quietude or lose anything through activity, in either case you have not yet reached the Way.

When you keep presence of mind, only then do you have autonomy. When you have autonomy, only then can you manage affairs. . . . However, presence of mind is easily interrupted. Practice it for a long time, though, and it will naturally become unbroken. Once it is unbroken, it is continuous. With continuity, the light shines bright. When the light shines bright, energy is full. When energy is full, then oblivion and distraction disappear without effort.

Observing mind means observing the purity of mind. The mind is basically nondual, just one vital reality; throughout the past and future, there is no other. Without leaving the objects of sense, you climb transcendent to the stage of enlightenment.

But observation of mind can be deep or shallow; there is forced observation and there is spontaneous observation. There is observation outside of sense objects, there is observation within sense objects; there is observation that is neither internal nor external, there is panoramic observation. With what observation do you observe mind?

When observation is deep and illusion is cleared, then this is true emptiness.

Turning the light around is done not by the eyes but by the mind; the mind is the eyes. After long persistence, the spirit congeals; only then do you see the mind-eyes become clear.

When you observe mind and become aware of openness, thereby you produce its vitality. When its vitality stabilizes, it becomes manifest, and then you see the opening of the mysterious pass.

Gazing at the lower abdomen is external work. As for the inner work, when the mind-eye comes into being, that alone is the true "elixir field."

The light you see before your eyes is rat-light, not the light of the tiger-eye or dragon-vitality. The light of mind does not belong to inside or outside; if you look to see it with the physical eyes, that is bedevilment.

You have been affected by pollution for so long that it is impossible to become clear all at once. In truth, the matter of life and death is important: once you turn the light around and recollect the vital spirit to shine stably, then your own mind is the lamp of enlightenment.

Everyone already has the lamp of mind, but it is necessary to light it so that it shines; then this is immortality.

Don't let yourselves forget the mind and allow the spirit to be obscured. If you have no autonomy, your vital spirit diffuses.

Forms are all conditioned. Cognition is a function of mind, empty silence is the substance of mind. If you fix the mind on anything conditioned, then temperament is in control, so you cannot govern it completely or comprehend it thoroughly.

The minor technique of circulating energy can enhance the body so as to extend the life span, but if you therefore suppose that the great Way requires work on the physical body, this is a tangential teaching.

External work has no connection to the great Way. The true practice of the great Way first requires that vitality be transformed into energy. As alchemical literature has clearly explained, this vitality is not sexual.

Refining energy into spirit means keeping the clear and removing the polluted.

Few are those who are calm and serious, rare are those who are sincere and unified.

Radiant light is the function of mind, empty silence is the substance of mind. If there is empty silence without radiant light, the silence is not true silence, the emptiness is not true emptiness—it is just a ghost cave.

The breathing that passes through the nose is external breathing, which is a phenomenon of the physical body. Only when mind and breathing rest on each other is this the true breath. The venerable Prajnatara [considered the twenty-seventh Indian ancestor of Chan Buddhism] said, "Breathing out, I do not follow myriad objects; breathing in, I do not dwell on the elements of body or mind." Is this the nose?

When it comes to watching the breathing, or listening to the breathing, these are still connected with the physical body. These are used to concentrate the mind and are not the real lifeline. The real lifeline is to be sought from within the real. Looking and listening are one thing.

The three realms are none other than your mind; your mind is not the three realms, yet it contains the three realms.

Whenever there is dependence, that is temporal; where there is no dependence, that is primal.

Where is the primal to be sought? It must be sought by way of the temporal. Temporal feelings and consciousness are marvelous functions of the primal. It must be sought through the work of practical balance in harmonious accord, which means calmness and openness. Of course, as long as clarification has not taken place, all is polluted. Clear up the pollution, and eventually there will be spontaneous clarity even without attempting to achieve clarity. Only then will the "gold pill" come out of the furnace.

When there is no self in the mind, it is even and clear; when the spirit is pure and the energy clear, this is Buddhahood and immortality. It is only because the iron pillars of thoughts are deeply rooted, and it is hard to escape their limitations, that it is necessary to observe one's own mind. When you see the mind, only then will you find the roots are insubstantial and thus have a sense of freedom from phenomena while having the ability to enter their range.

The primal and temporal are originally not two: what makes the distinction is only temporal. When you discriminate, then action and stillness are not united, and primal energy becomes conditioned. When they are united, temporal energy is also primal, and there is no distinction between primal and temporal.

If there is discrimination between primal and temporal, that is just consciousness; if you discriminate, then conditioning flares up, and this is the source of the profuse confusion of thoughts.

What cannot be spoken and cannot be named is the generative energy, which is the substance of the Way. When the substance is established, the function operates.

When people are deluded by emotions and do not know there is essence, they are ordinary ignoramuses. If they know there is essence but do not know there are emotions, this is senseless vacuity. Therefore our teaching is actively living and does not settle into one corner, but instead applies to heaven and earth, combines eternity with the present, equalizes others and self, and has neither enemy nor familiar.

It is said that we are the same in essence but different in feeling. There is no difference in feeling either; it is just that habits develop unnoticed, evolving in a stream, continuing to the present, so that their defiling influence cannot be shed. Ultimately this is not the fault of essence.

The great Way is not in quiet living. If you stay quietly in a room, that has the countereffect of increasing the flames of fire in the heart. It is necessary to be working on the Way whatever you are doing in order to be able to "sit on the summit of a thousand mountains without leaving the crossroads."

Consciousness is knowledge. In ordinary people it is called consciousness, in immortals and Buddhas it is called knowledge. The only distinction is between purity and impurity.

The noncognizing in the consciousness is the eternal; the consciousness in noncognizing is wisdom. If you arouse a discriminatory, galloping mind, this is routine, and you become an ordinary mortal.

How can you find purity in the mind? It is just a matter of seeking out purity in the midst of impurity. Then when you discover signs of impurity in the midst of purity, you have now found purity.

The true mind has no form: what has form is ultimately illusory.

Is the true mind to be sought from the source of mind? If the source is clean, then the celestial design is apparent, and daily activities never obstruct the supreme Way. If the source is not clean, then even if you have some vision it is like a lamp in the wind, flickering erratically.

What we call the true mind is the enlightened clear mind. Therefore it can pervade the heavens and permeate the earth, without the slightest artificiality.

When mind is empty yet not vacant, this is called true emptiness; when mind is there but not reified, this is called subtle existence. Don't tarry on one side, and you then enter the middle way. Then you have a basis for gaining access to virtue.

The Way is present before our eyes, yet what is before our eyes is hard to understand. People like the unusual and enjoy the new; they miss what is right in front of their eyes and do not know where the Way is. The Way is the immediate presence: if you are unaware of the immediate presence, then your mind races, your intellect runs, and you go on thinking compulsively. All of this is due to shallowness of spiritual power, and shallowness of spiritual power is due to racing in the mind.

Translation Notes

I. The Celestial Mind

1. The identification of the Way with essence and primal spirit follows the traditions of the Chan school of Buddhism and the northern branch of the Completely Real school of Taoism.

2. Essence is open and spacious, like the sky; life is a quantity of energy, like light. When the text talks about the two eyes guiding attention, it means that both spacelike awareness and specific perception are operative at the same time.

3. This passage introduces the idea of a succession of transmitters of the teaching of the golden flower, to link it with the Way of the ancients.

4. The honorific name Taishang (T'ai-shang) refers to the metaphysical reality represented by Lao-tzu, legendary author of *Tao Te Ching,* the basic classic of Taoism. Donghua (Tung-hua) was the teacher of Zhongli Quan (Chung-li Ch'uan), who was the teacher of Lu Yan (Lu Yen). Lu Yan is the "Yan" mentioned in our text; he is regarded as the immediate ancestor of the Completely Real (Quanzhen /Ch'uan-chen) school of Taoism, which was founded by his disciples and descendants in the eleventh and twelfth centuries.

The teaching of the golden flower itself is attributed to Lu Yan. There are numerous conflicting stories about the life and times of Lu Yan, but in Taoist tradition it is widely believed that he attained immortality and is still alive. Most of the texts attributed to Lu Yan were received by spiritual communications centuries after the founding of the Complete Reality school and were not written by Lu himself.

5. Completely Real Taoism became so influential in the twelfth and thirteenth centuries that it attracted many opportunistic followers and imitators. Later many practices originally abandoned by the school were amalgamated with elements of Completely Real Taoism to produce bastardized forms. At the time of the writing of our text, approximately 250 years ago, Completely Real Taoism was almost entirely a name without a reality.

6. "Master Siu" seems to refer to Xu Jingyang (Hsu Ching-yang), a great Taoist of the third and fourth centuries who is said to have foretold the appearance of Lu Yan, to whom this text is attributed. He is also believed to have said he would reappear in the world twelve centuries later, which would have been shortly before *The Secret of the Golden Flower* is supposed to have been received from Lu Yan. This text is said to be a written form of a teaching that was originally wordless, an esoteric component of the movement received during a period of special concentration. The term *special transmission outside of doctrine* is a byword of Chan Buddhism. The practice of contemplative vigils like the one in which the golden flower teaching was revealed is also a standard exercise of latter-day Chan Buddhism.

7. The foregoing passages on the lineage of the text were omitted in Richard Wilhelm's translation. These passages are rather laconic, and someone with Wilhelm's knowledge

of Chinese language and Taoist history could hardly have been expected to be able to interpret them. It is not clear, however, why Wilhelm also excised paragraph 7 on the importance of an orderly life as a prerequisite for the mystical practice of the golden flower. It may not have conformed sufficiently to his idea of mysticism. Westerners have often professed to believe that mystics are generally isolated from society, and this opinion has affected many Western attempts to interpret and adopt mystical teachings.

8. The speaker is supposed to be Lu Yan, or Ancestor Lu, whom later Taoist texts envision as having been entrusted with a mission for the celestial government and duty-bound to reappear in the human world from time to time.

9. Wilhelm completely mistranslates this passage, making it out to say the very opposite of what it actually does. This appears to be mostly due to simple misunderstanding of the language and unfamiliarity with the background of the text. The passage describes the distinctive nature of the text as representing a sudden enlightenment teaching, in contrast to the gradual teachings of ordinary Taoist works on spiritual alchemy. This identifies the Chan Buddhist influence behind the Taoist facade of the text.

10. "The lead in the homeland of water is just one flavor" comes from *Understanding Reality,* the great classic of the Completely Real school. Lead symbolizes the true sense of real knowledge. Water stands for a symbol from the ancient *I Ching* representing the true sense of the knowledge of reality enclosed within conscious knowledge. To say that it is just one flavor means that it is attained by the essence of consciousness itself, not by any modification of consciousness. This is what makes it truly universal and unlimited by sectarian or cultural discriminations.

11. The expression "turning the light around" refers to the Chan Buddhist exercise of mentally looking inward toward the source of consciousness. Wilhelm translates this as "circulation of the light," which is not very plausible linguistically but nevertheless could have been an honest mistake. Evidently he confused this with the waterwheel exercise of Taoist energetics, in which a quantity of psychic heat would be consciously conducted along a certain route through the body.

Many cultists imitated this exercise on the level of fixated attention without the psychic heat and noticed the characteristic modifications of consciousness these postures produce. It is quite possible that Wilhelm got this idea from a member of such a cult. The notes added to the *Golden Flower* text he used (which was printed some two hundred years after the movement had arisen) tend to dilute the Chan with materials that make it look like a run-of-the mill mixture of alchemy and energetics. Wilhelm's medical training also seems to have predisposed him to make physiological interpretations

There is evidence to suggest that it was possible to read certain special mind-body postures of attention into portions of the original text. These postures were used only for temporarily anchoring the mind while performing the inner gazing toward the source of consciousness. This is not the same as the energy circulation of Taoist practice. The text speaks of the highest experiences being purely mental, "in the heart," elevating the spiritual over the physical in the manner of Chan Buddhism and the northern branch of Completely Real Taoism.

12. The celestial mind refers to unconditioned consciousness; light is its function. When the light is "turned around" and directed toward its own source, environmental and psycho-

logical factors influence the mind less, with the result that the energy in the body is also preserved and purified because it is not drawn into conflicts with inner or outer states.

13. The expression "above the nine skies" means a state of mind beyond the influence of mundane conditioning. In Buddhist terminology it also has the special meaning of being above all cultivated meditation states. *Silently paying court (to God)* and *soaring upward* are common Taoist expressions for elevation of consciousness. There are several *Mind Seal* scriptures, and it is not certain to which of these the text refers in this passage.

14. Taoist master Liu I-ming says of the gold pill, "The pill is the original, primal, real unified energy. This energy, when passed through fire to refine it, becomes permanently indestructible, so it is called the gold pill."

II. The Original Spirit and the Conscious Spirit

1. The distinction between the original spirit and the conscious spirit is one of the most important ideas in Taoist psychology. The conscious spirit is historically conditioned; the original spirit is primal and universal. The conscious spirit is a complex of modifications of awareness, while the original spirit is the essence of awareness. To say that this essence transcends the "primal organization" means that it is by nature more fundamental than even the most basic patterns of modification to which consciousness may be subject. In Jungian terms, this means that the essence of the original spirit is beyond, or deeper than, even the archetypes of the collective unconscious. Jung himself does not seem to have attained this, and his work reflects what

in Taoist terms would be termed confusion of the conscious spirit (which includes the Jungian "unconscious") with the original spirit.

2. Vitality, energy, and spirit are the fundamental triad of being, known in Taoist terms as the "three treasures" of the human body. Here the spirit is the only one regarded as transcendental. This is characteristic of Buddhistic neo-Taoist spiritual immortalism, which tends to deemphasize the physiological practices of old alchemical immortalism. To "live transcendentally outside of yin and yang" means to be aloof from the ups and downs of ordinary life in the midst of changes in the world.

    Three realms is a Buddhist term. The realms are the domains of desire, form, and formlessness, representing the totality of conditioned experience, from the coarsest to the most subtle. Wilhelm, who seems to have known little about Buddhism, writes in a note that the three realms, or "three worlds," as he translates them, are "Heaven, earth, and hell." Jung's work on archetypes and dreams would have benefited immensely from an accurate understanding of the real Buddhist concept of three realms or worlds. As it was, Jung does not seem to have been able to distinguish these realms of experience clearly; most of his work appears to hover on the border of the realms of form and desire; the realm of formless consciousness seems to have been unfamiliar to him. Perhaps Wilhelm's Christian background influenced his interpretation of this term.

3. *Seeing essence* and *original face* are both Chan Buddhist terms, here used to refer to the Taoist experience of the primal spirit. It is evident that Wilhelm was not familiar with even the most rudimentary lore of Chan Buddhism.

4. This passage refers to a certain stage that is often referred to

in Taoist yogic texts in much more physical terms than it is here, where the Chan Buddhist/northern Complete Reality influence is again manifest. Wilhelm's translation of "instincts and movements" for "on the verge of moving into action" misconstrues both Chinese grammar and the nature of the experience to which the passage refers. When the text speaks of this as a secret that "has not been transmitted in a thousand ages," it means that the experience can only be understood firsthand.

5. Chan Buddhism traditionally describes the mechanism of delusion as mistaking the servant for the master. In the metaphor of this passage, the general is supposed to be a servant but instead usurps authority. According to Chan/Taoist psychology, the conscious mind (which does the thinking) is supposed to be a servant of the original mind, but the activity of the conscious mind tends to become so self-involved that it seems to have become an independent entity. When "the sword is turned around," in the metaphor of our text, the original mind retrieves command over the delinquent conscious mind.

6. The "chamber of the origin" means the source of awareness; keeping to the chamber of the origin is turning around the light of consciousness to be aware of its own source. In this way the mind is freed from compulsive concern with its own productions. Through this practice it becomes possible to control and order the conscious mind without force, by maintaining the central position of the original mind.

Like many Western interpreters of his time, Jung had the idea that yoga involves or produces abnormal psychic states and is aimed at total detachment from the external world, or at transcendental unity without differentiation.

In the real *Golden Flower* teaching there is no suggestion of obliterating the conscious mind (which in this context means the mind that thinks, imagines, dreams, and emotes, including what Jung called the unconscious).

The faculties of thinking, imagining, dreaming, and emotion are not destroyed in the earthly immortal of Taoism; rather they are brought under the dominion of their source of power and made into channels of its expression. The taming of unruly consciousness is far from the introverted, quietistic cult that Wilhelm, Jung, and others of their time imagined from their fragmentary observations of Eastern lore.

7. Wilhelm translates "the water of vitality" as "seed-water" and equates it with Eros; he translates "the fire of spirit" as "spirit-fire" and equates it with Logos; and he translates "the earth of attention" as "thought-earth" and equates it with intuition. Of these three, Eros is closest to certain Taoist meanings of vitality, in the sense of creative energy and erotic feeling. In this context, however, Eros is inappropriate in that the meaning of vitality here does not include erotic feeling. Even the connection with creative energy is actually remote in this text, because the real meaning here is the sense of true knowledge of the original mind. This can be known from the symbolism of water as explained in the following text.

    As for "spirit-fire" and Logos, this seems even less appropriate, since the fire of spirit here just means awareness and does not at this point differentiate between the original spirit and the conscious spirit. The sacred and the profane are mixed, and the spirit does not deserve the name of Logos yet. This is the very reason for the alchemy: to refine the sacred, pure primal spirit out of the profane, conditioned conscious spirit.

The earth of attention is translated by Wilhelm as "thought-earth" and identified with intuition, but thought and intuition properly belong to the realm symbolized by fire, not that of earth. Water and fire, real knowledge and conscious knowledge, primal unity and present awareness, are brought together in the medium of earth, which stands for attention, concentration, intent, or will. Here it is identified with the celestial mind, which means that it is innocent of temporal conditioning.

In other texts this is called pure attention or true intent. Since earth is the medium, it must be purified before it can absorb the pure essences of water and fire to combine them. If the focus of attention is itself already biased by the activity of an unruly consciousness, then it may not be able to draw that consciousness to an orderly reality of which it is as yet unconscious.

8. The "energy of the primal real unity" stands for the living flux of the perpetual cycles of natural evolution, wherein all beings and all things live in the lives of one another. *The Book of Balance and Harmony,* an ancient text of the Complete Reality school antedating the golden flower dispensation by over four hundred years, expresses the idea of the primal unity in these terms: "All beings are basically one form and one energy. Form and energy are basically one spirit. Spirit is basically utter openness. The Tao is basically ultimate nonbeing. Change is therein." The combination of water and fire in the medium of earth thus refers to experiential realization of the unity of being from a transcendental point of view that is changeless itself yet accommodates all change.

9. Wilhelm used the terms Eros, Logos, and intuition in an attempt to convey the Chinese ideas to a Western audience,

but the assignments he made are largely subjective and arbitrary from the point of view of Chinese Taoist tradition. Part of the problem seems to be that as a Christian he understood the Chinese word "spirit" to be associated with either the divine or the supernatural.

In the first section of this text, for example, Wilhelm translates *zhixu zhiling zhi shen,* which means a spirit (i.e., mind) that is completely open and completely effective, as "God of Utmost Emptiness and Life." Based on this sort of translation, Jung thought that the Chinese had no idea that they were discussing psychological phenomena. He then tried to repsychologize the terminology, but since he did not quite understand it to begin with he could not but wind up with a distortion in the end.

It is little wonder that Jung came to imagine, through his own attempts at meditation, that the Taoists had arrived at the entrance to the science of psychology "only through abnormal psychic states," as he wrote in his commentary to Wilhelm's version of *The Secret of the Golden Flower.* It is worth noting in this connection that Jung also found late medieval baroque Christian alchemical books puzzling but did not openly accuse their authors of having come upon their science through induction of aberrated mental states.

10. The concepts of the higher and lower souls were among those that caught the special attention of Wilhelm and Jung in connection with their Christian backgrounds and interests. Wilhelm uses the term *anima* for lower soul and *animus* for higher soul. In his introduction he deemphasizes the gender associations of yin and yang, but in connection with the concept of the souls Wilhelm calls the anima feminine and the animus masculine. Jung then proceeds to exaggerate this distortion even further in his

own disquisition on feminine and masculine psychologies. None of this gets to the heart of the discussion of our text.

The idea that the body is created by attention is typically Buddhist, but it is also found in the schools of Taoism influenced by Buddhism. In this text, the "lower soul" simply means the feeling of being a solid body physically present in a solid world. As long as this feeling persists, the state of the lower soul (which includes visceral emotions) is subject to random environmental influences. Therefore the text speaks of "interrupting consciousness" in the sense of withdrawing attention from the feeling of solidity in order to free it from the bonds of external influences, making it less sticky and more fluid, unbounded by temporal events.

11. In colloquial Chinese usage, "liver and heart" means what is essential. In a human being, the liver is associated with courage and conscience. This passage illustrates the Taoist awareness of the connection between waking and dreaming experience.

12. The nine heavens and nine earths stand for the whole universe of experience, from the most exalted to the most profound.

13. This passage connects the last three: the process of the exercise is to turn attention around to the source of awareness to refine the higher soul, thus preserve the spirit, thus control the lower soul, and thus interrupt the conditioned stream of consciousness. The purpose of interrupting the stream of consciousness is described in the following passage.

14. "Dissolving the lower soul" means detachment from the feeling of physical existence. As the text subsequently makes clear, there is no real lower soul that is in substance

different from the higher soul. They are both aspects of one spirit, artificially alienated by confusion. When energy is freed from obsessive clinging to the body or lower soul, it can be used to restore the original spirit to completeness.

15. Turning the light around, or directing attention toward the source of awareness, counteracts the tendency to dwell on objects or modifications of consciousness. Here this is called "dissolving darkness and controlling the lower soul."

    Taoists use a symbol from the *I Ching* known as *heaven* or *the creative* to represent what Chan Buddhists call the original face or the mind ground. When the text says that other than turning the light around there is no special exercise for restoring this primal wholeness, it confirms that the practice being taught is that of Northern Taoism as influenced by Chan Buddhism, and not the physiological energetics of Southern Taoism as influenced by Tantric Buddhism.

16. The term *embryo of sagehood* or *embryonic enlightenment* is very common in classical Chan Buddhist texts of the Tang and Sung dynasties. It seems to have passed into Complete Reality Taoism from Chan, but a parallel idea occurs in certain pre-Chan Taoist scriptures. The formation of the embryo represents the initial awakening of the mind. *Nurturing the embryo,* a term frequently found in Chan, refers to the process of development and maturation after awakening.

17. "Concentrating the spirit on where the celestial mind rests when the embryo leaves the shell" is a typical Chan Buddhist formulation, here expressed in the terminology of Taoism. The Northern Taoist master Liu I-ming also uses the metaphor of the dung beetle in his *Awakening to the Tao,* where he uses it similarly to describe the creation of

the transcendent being by concentration of spirit: "In the midst of ecstatic trance there is a point of living potential, coming into being from nonbeing, whereby the spiritual embryo can be formed and the spiritual body be produced."

18. This passage shows that the division of so-called higher and lower souls is regarded as not a primal metaphysical reality but a temporal psychic phenomenon. When the text says that the light, clear energy characteristic of the higher soul is "obtained from cosmic space," it refers to the equanimous spacelike awareness taught in Chan Buddhism and Complete Reality Taoism. This spacelike awareness contains everything while resting on nothing; it is the basic experience of the Chan master or Taoist wizard who lives in the midst of the things of the world yet is free from bondage to them. This contrasts with the limitation of awareness represented by the lower soul, mixed up in the objects of its perception.

    Since Jung's "collective unconscious" still has form, from the point of view of the golden flower it must therefore be classified with the lower soul and ordinary mind; his hope was to make this conscious in order to transcend it, but Jung himself appears to have become so involved in the discovery and discussion of the unconscious that he became attached to it and as a consequence was never able to experience the higher soul and open the golden flower. His commentary on Wilhelm's translation bears witness to this, as do his other writings on Eastern mysticism.

19. Here life means spirit, and death means matter. Feeding on blood is emblematic of attachment to the body as self, carried through the very portals of physical death. According to Chan Buddhist psychology, what are mythologically

portrayed as experiences of hell after death are in fact manifestations of this attachment wrenching the heart as one is dying. When this text speaks of a "coming together of kind," it means that whatever attention is fixated on material things inevitably meets the fate of all material things, which is to perish and decay.

20. This final passage again drives home the point that the lower soul has no independent existence but is just a conditioned modification of the original "unified awareness" and can therefore be changed and refined to a point at which it is also pragmatically no different from the higher soul. This refinement is the object of the practice of turning the light around taught in this *Golden Flower* text.

III. Turning the Light Around and Keeping to the Center

1. The Taoist adept Wenshi (Wen-shih) was believed to be a student of Lao-tzu, transmitter of the classic *Tao Te Ching*. A text known as *The True Scripture of Wenshi* says, "Our Way is like being in darkness. Those in the light cannot see a single thing in the darkness, whereas those who are in darkness can see everything in the light."

2. "Nonbeing within being" refers to a sense of openness and spaciousness in the midst of things, which is first produced by the exercise of turning the light around. "Being within nonbeing" refers to the presence of energy within the vastness of the mind merged with space. The "body beyond your body" refers to the hidden reserve of vital energy uncovered by the opening of the mind.

3. The period of a hundred days is commonly mentioned in Taoist texts as the length of time required to set up the

foundation by stabilizing the concentration of consciousness. The actual time may naturally be different; the criterion is the production of the effect. The term *firing process* is also taken from Taoist spiritual alchemy and means the course of meditation work, symbolized by the firing or cooking of elixir to crystallize it into a pill.

4. "Positive light" means the creative energy in the original mind. The "eyes" are the two main aspects of consciousness symbolized by sky and light: formless awareness and awareness of form. "Running leakage" means that energy is wasted through involvement with objects. This is called "conformity" because it happens as a matter of course when the mind is conditioned by things. "Reversal" therefore means withdrawing energy from objects, so that it can be stabilized and mastered from within rather than controlled from without.

5. Turning the light around is turning around the energy of creation in that the total experience of the world depends upon the orientation of the mind. Changsha, a distinguished Chan master of the ninth century, is famous for saying, "All worlds in the ten directions are the light of the self. All worlds in the ten directions are in the light of the self. In all worlds in the ten directions, there is no one who is not oneself. I always tell people that the Buddhas of past, present, and future, together with the sentient beings of the whole universe, are the light of great wisdom. Before the light radiates, where do you place it? Before the light radiates, there is not even a trace of Buddhas or sentient beings—where do you find the mountains, rivers, and lands?"

    This exercise stops random imagination and empties routine compulsion by stopping them at the source. The teaching of Pure Land Buddhism expresses a similar experience by saying that one single-minded recollection of the Buddha of Infinite Light erases eighty eons of sins. The idea is that habits of false thought exist only to the extent that they are continually tended, groomed, and renewed. Deprived of center-stage attention, these habits lose their power over the mind.

6. Being rhythmical, breathing is thought of as going through four seasons with each breath. One of the founders of the Complete Reality school describes the intensification of time in the process of spiritual incubation in Taoist alchemy as the experience of the mental equivalent of thirty-six thousand years within one year of concentration. This represents a process of accelerated conscious evolution.

7. Here "conformity" is defined as pursuing objects. The idea of a "netherworld" is not confined in this context to a state after death, but stands for a condition of depletion in which there is no more creativity left and one lives through sheer force of habit.

   The *Heroic March Scripture* is a Buddhist text that came into vogue among Chan contemplatives in the tenth or eleventh century. It has continued in popularity because of its detailed descriptions of meditation states, highly valued in the absence of expert teachers. Eventually certain formulations of this scripture were also taken over by Taoist yogis borrowing techniques from Buddhism.

8. The *Yin Convergence Classic (Yinfu jing)* and the *Plain Questions of the Yellow Emperor (Huang Di suwen jing)* are Taoist texts, both considered very old. The former work is also attributed to the Yellow Emperor mentioned in the title of the latter. This legendary figure of high antiquity is one of the great cultural heroes of Taoism and Chinese culture in

general. One type of Taoism, called the Huang-Lao teaching after the names of the mythical founders known as Yellow Emperor (Huang Di) and Lao-tzu, was ostensibly concerned with immortalism.

Note that here "long life" and "transcendence of life" are presented as rooted in psychological experience. It is common among Complete Reality Taoists to understand immortality as higher consciousness, with no necessary relation to the longevity of the physical body as measured in terrestrial time. Nevertheless, the mental ease resulting from the experience of spiritual "immortality" is also said to generally preserve and enhance physical health by freeing the individual from destructive stress and tension.

9. The "three teachings" are Taoism, Buddhism, and Confucianism. From its very inception, the Complete Reality school of Taoism has taught that these three philosophies share a common essence. This was accepted by Buddhists, especially the Chan contemplatives, but Confucians were averse to recognize any affinity with Buddhism even as they absorbed Chan methodology into their own studies. Wilhelm translates this passage, "This is the common goal of all religions," and in his introduction he notes that Taoist organizations included not only Confucians, Taoists, and Buddhists but also Muslims, Christians, and Jews.

10. Jung used the concepts of introversion and extroversion to describe what he thought were characteristic attitudes of Eastern and Western mentalities. He absorbed himself in his own fantasy world, and he imagined that the Chinese Taoists did the same thing. Since our text says, however, that "the light is neither inside nor outside the self," it can hardly be supposed that turning the light around is the same thing as introversion in the Jungian sense. The

Chan/Taoist meditative exercise of turning the light around does not make one oblivious of the external world, nor does it by any means involve concern with images or fantasies that may occur to the mind.

11. Quiet sitting was commonly practiced by Buddhists, Taoists, and neo-Confucians. *The Book of Balance and Harmony,* a compendium of all three teachings as they were practiced in the Completely Real school of Taoism, says, "What the three teachings esteem is calm stability. This is called being based on calm. When the human mind is calm and stable, unaffected by things, it is merged in the celestial design."

12. The state where "heaven is open, earth is broad, and all things are just as they are" is described in graphic detail by the nineteenth-century Completely Real Taoist master Liu I-ming in his *Awakening to the Tao,* wherein he speaks of emulating heaven and earth: "If people can be open minded and magnanimous, be receptive to all, take pity on the old and the poor, assist those in peril and rescue those in trouble, give of themselves without seeking reward, never bear grudges, look upon others and self impartially, and realize all as one, then people can be companions of heaven. If people can be flexible and yielding, humble, with self-control, free of agitation, clear of volatility, not angered by criticism, ignoring insult, docilely accepting all hardships, illnesses, and natural disasters, without anxiety or resentment when faced with danger or adversity, then people can be companions of earth. With the nobility of heaven and the humility of earth, one joins in with the attributes of heaven and earth and extends to eternity with them."

13. "Reversed gazing" means turning attention to the source of awareness; it is one of the standard expressions of the golden flower technique. *Reaching toward knowledge* is a special

Taoist usage of a Confucian term. Originally it meant attaining knowledge by assessment of things. Here it is used to stand for the exercise of "turning the light around" and reaching toward the source of knowing. There are many examples of special Taoist uses of Confucian and Buddhist terms to be found in the literature of syncretic schools such as that of the Golden Flower.

There follow in Wilhelm's translation six paragraphs that are not in the Chinese text available to me. Their content marks them as interpolations or footnotes.

14. *Small Stopping and Seeing* is a classic compendium of basic meditation techniques, composed by the founder of Tiantai Buddhism in the sixth century A.D. Wilhelm does not translate this passage, and he misconstrues the terms *stopping* and *seeing* as "fixating contemplation." The terms mean stopping random thought and seeing successive layers of truth. This recommendation of a popular Buddhist meditation guidebook as a "touchstone" illustrates the close relationship between Buddhist and Taoist contemplative practices of the time.

15. "Focus on the center" is translated by Wilhelm as "the center in the midst of conditions," misreading the verb *yuan*, "focus," as the noun *yuan*, "condition." There follows a passage (not in my Chinese text) interpreting "focus on the center" to mean, as Wilhelm translates, "fixing one's thinking on the point which lies exactly between the two eyes." This is not what the Buddhist term originally means, and this consciousness-altering technique in Wilhelm's version is the subject of strong warnings in modern literature of the Completely Real school of Taoism; it is said to be very dangerous.

The presence of numerous such fragmentary yogic interpolations out of character with the overall teaching of the text leads me to suspect that Wilhelm's text had been doctored by quasi-Taoist cultists, quite possibly disaffected Confucians, who were devoted or addicted to altered states of consciousness.

The meaning of the "center" in the context of Complete Reality Taoism is more accurately defined by Liu I-ming in my *I Ching Mandalas:* "The spirit of openness is the center. The mysterious female is essence and life. The immortality of the spirit of openness is the center containing essence and life. Setting up the foundation on the mysterious female is essence and life constituting the center. Those who keep to this center are sages, those who lose this center are ordinary mortals."

As to the center being the "mechanism of Creation," Liu says, "The center is the great root of the world. All the sages, immortals, and Buddhas of all times are born from this center. It is so vast that there is nothing outside it, yet so minute that it retreats into storage in secrecy. Those who awaken to this immediately ascend to the ranks of sages, while those who miss this are sunk for eons."

Liu also affirms the subtlety of the center, and the delicacy of the mental posture of focus on the center, to which he denies any physical location as suggested by Wilhelm's version of the *Golden Flower* text. Liu says: "It has no location, no fixed position. Look for it and you cannot see it, listen for it and you cannot hear it. Try to grasp it and you cannot find it. . . . It is not easy for people to see this center, and not easy for them to know it. It cannot be consciously sought, it cannot be mindlessly kept. If you seek it consciously, you fall into forms; if you keep it mindlessly, you enter into empty silence. Neither of these is the central way."

In *I Ching Mandalas* Liu specifically repudiates interpretations in terms of yogic exercises such as that described in

Wilhelm's text, emphasizing the dangers inherent in such practices: "Students everywhere are ignorant of just what this center is. Some say it is the center of the body, some say it is the center of the top of the head, some say it is the region of the heart, some say it is the center of the forehead, some say it is the throat, some say it is in the middle of the space between the kidneys and genitals. Vainly hoping for eternal life, they cling to points in this ephemeral body and call that keeping to the center and embracing the one. Not only will they not live eternally, they will even hasten death."

16. This passage is seriously misconstrued in Wilhelm's version. When the text says, "Hereafter, whenever thoughts arise, you don't need to sit still as before," it is referring to the time after the hundred days' work of setting up the foundation, during which the power of introspective concentration is stabilized. Investigating the locus of thought, where it arises and passes away, is a method of turning the light around commonly practiced in later Chan Buddhism.

Here and following, Wilhelm translates "need not" as "must not," and "cannot be grasped" as "cannot be done." These misconstructions thoroughly skew the meaning, because they miss the effective thrust of the text. The point of the exercise is to experience the ungraspability of mind in itself. Where the text says "Push this inquiry on and on over and over until you realize it cannot be grasped," Wilhelm translates, "Nothing is gained by pushing reflection further," which is completely off the mark; it would be impossible to attain the true effect of the practice following Wilhelm's version. What he renders as "nothing is gained" is a very common Buddhist expression meaning "ungraspable."

When the text says, "'Having looked for my mind, I realize it cannot be grasped.' 'I have pacified your mind for you,'" it alludes to one of the most famous of Chan Buddhist stories. A seeker asked the founder of Chan to pacify his mind. The Chan founder said, "Bring me your mind and I will pacify it for you." The seeker said, "Having looked for my mind, I realize it cannot be grasped." The founder said, "I have pacified your mind for you." This illustrates the climax of the exercise of turning the light around. Wilhelm had apparently never read or heard this story.

17. "Once you reach this ungraspability" is translated by Wilhelm as "That leads to no goal." In many cases Wilhelm does not seem to have been able to decipher the text well enough even to discern where a sentence begins or ends. He also translates "stopping" as "fixating," but fixation is definitely proscribed in the instructions of this very same text.

18. The canonical Chinese text ends the section here; Wilhelm's includes a rather long discourse on yogic technique, which he treats as an addition separate from the main text. The content of the interpolated passages points to a fairly typical kind of cultism and mentions practices that are popular but dangerous. It is worth reemphasizing this danger, for such practices are also found in other popular books on Taoism in English, without the warnings that accompany their mention in authentic Chinese Taoist books. These exercises are in fact unnecessary for the practice of turning the light around as taught in the real golden flower doctrine.

IV. Turning the Light Around and Tuning the Breathing

1. Chan Buddhism teaches that realization comes of itself and cannot be anticipated because it is not a product of subjec-

tive imagination. Hopes and expectations on the part of the practitioner inhibit the spontaneous working of the potential that makes realization possible.

2. Oblivion and distraction are commonly treated in Buddhist meditation manuals as the two main "sicknesses" to which meditators are prone. Focusing the mind on the breathing is an ancient Buddhist practice that is especially popular among modern-day Zennists. *Spiritual Alchemy for Women,* a late-nineteenth-century Taoist work, says, "In general, what is most essential at the beginning of this study is self-refinement. Self-refinement is a matter of mind and breathing resting on each other. This means that the mind rests on the breathing and the breathing rests on the mind" (from *Immortal Sisters*).

3. Taoists and Buddhists both observe the intimate natural connection between breathing and mental state. When the mind is excited, the breathing accelerates; when the mind is calm, so is the breath. The practice of resting mind and breath on each other makes deliberate use of this relationship to calm the mind down and gradually bring it to a state of stillness.

4. "Inward breathing" is the rhythm of consciousness, "outward breathing" is the rhythm of respiration. Taoists and Buddhists both use the image of "leaking" to represent the loss of energy through random mental activity and its corresponding physical unrest. Buddhas and Taoist immortals are described as having "put an end to leakage."

5. Taoist and Buddhist texts describe many manifestations of human tendencies toward polarization and extremism. These include notices of people trying to stop thinking completely, believing this to be the goal of meditation

practice. In Taoist literature there is also mention of people who even try to stop breathing. The idea of "making the affliction itself into medicine" is characteristically Buddhist, also described in later Taoist literature as "temporarily using things of the world to cultivate principles of the Way."

6. Here the "light of the eyes" refers to awareness of the world at large, while the "light of the ears" refers to formless inner awareness. Here again the text makes it clear that there is no real boundary or difference between inside and outside: "They have the same source, but different names" (*Tao Te Ching*). The practice of "turning back to the nature of hearing," which is one way of turning the light around, comes from the *Heroic March Scripture,* a Buddhist text popular among latter-day Chan Buddhist contemplatives and figuring prominently in the technical procedures outlined in the *Golden Flower* text.

7. To "let go" is to free the mind from entanglement in objects, but to "let go absolutely" is to fall into oblivion. Again the balance of "stopping" and "seeing" is critical to the success of the exercise.

8. Taoist texts distinguish several levels of refinement according to sound, but soundless breathing is considered best of all. Six audible breaths are used for healing, while silent breathing is used for quiet meditation. Since mental silence is considered the best hygiene as well as the best curative, soundlessly subtle breathing is generally considered very important for both mental and physical aspects of Taoist practice.

9. The term *true breathing* is variously defined in Taoist literature; sometimes it is represented as respiration that is so subtle that it is completely unnoticeable, sometimes it is

represented as the inner rhythm of awareness ordinarily obscured by the coarseness of thinking.

10. This passage makes it clear that practice of resting mind and breathing on each other is just a starting point. Such concentration exercises are only temporary expedients, but cultists sometimes perform them routinely for years on end. A famous Chan poem says, "When the wine is always sweet, it lays out the guests," meaning that overindulgence in concentration and consequent addiction to calmness can actually incapacitate the individual for further development.

11. *The Book of Balance and Harmony* says, "By keeping energy complete you can nurture the mind. To keep energy complete first requires that the mind be clear and calm. When clear and calm, there are no thoughts, so energy is complete."

12.-13. The metaphor of the hen incubating an egg is commonly used in Chan Buddhism to represent continuous attention.

14. *The Book of Balance and Harmony* says, "Of old it has been said, always extinguish the stirring mind, don't extinguish the shining mind. The unstirring mind is the shining mind, the mind that does not stop is the wandering mind."

16.-20. It is so much easier to notice distraction when sitting quietly than when engaged in activity that people often feel their minds to be more scattered than usual when they begin to sit quietly. Oblivion is a much more difficult problem, not only because of its nature as unawareness but also because contemplatives are often unconsciously attracted to it. Distraction, in contrast, is so annoying that it naturally provokes the desire to overcome it. Therefore Taoism traditionally emphasizes the importance of using both stillness and movement in developmental exercises, to avoid falling into either extreme.

23.–27. Not looking or listening does not mean not seeing or hearing. It is a matter of being spontaneous rather than contrived. The text again makes it clear that this is not introversion as understood by Jungian psychology. In particular, paragraph 27 shows that this practice is not a matter of attention to subconscious mental activity, as Jung seemed to think.

28. Fixing the length of time for meditation can have negative effects, turning what is supposed to be a liberative technique into an automatizing ritual. Japanese Zennists and their Western imitators often seem to think of sitting meditation in quantitative terms, but in the golden flower teaching quality is the foremost consideration. According to National Teacher Muso Soseki, one of the early greats of Japanese Zen, the establishment of fixed periods of sitting meditation was originally a matter of discipline, instituted during the Middle Ages to cope with large numbers of monastic inmates who had entered Zen orders for economic or sociological reasons.

V. Errors in Turning the Light Around

1. "There are many pitfalls in front of the cliff of withered trees" is an adaptation of a Chan Buddhist saying. The cliff of withered trees stands for a state of nonthinking quiescence, from which standpoint it is easy to fall unawares into deviations. Wilhelm translates "in front of the cliff of withered trees" as "before you reach the condition where you sit like a withered tree before a cliff." This may give the

misleading impression that the "withered tree" condition is the goal.

2. Chan Buddhism tended to become increasingly simplistic as time went on, and it was generally not systematized to the same degree as Taoist alchemy. There was also a traditional reluctance in Chan Buddhism to speak much about psychic states.

4. This passage combines Taoist and Chan Buddhist warnings against quietism. "Don't sit inside nothingness or indifference" is a common Chan Buddhist expression. Wilhelm misconstrues it as "One must not sit down (to meditate) in the midst of frivolous affairs," which is in a sense antithetical to the actual meaning of the expression. The Buddhist term *neutral voidness* is inserted in a note in the original text.

5. This is another caution against quietism or nihilism; "letting go" is not to be exaggerated into oblivion.

6. Both Completely Real Taoism and Chan Buddhism commonly warn against becoming enthusiastic or excited in anticipating experiences in meditation, since this agitates the mind and stimulates subjective projections, thus retarding progress. Wilhelm translates, "Nor must the thoughts be concentrated on the right procedure." This is a misreading of the words, and a misleading idea.

   The parenthetical comments in my translation are also notes in the original text. "You can get it by intent that is not willful" is translated by Wilhelm as "If one can attain purposelessness through purpose." It is not clear what he thought this meant. The idea of "purposelessness" seems to have appealed to C. G. Jung insofar as he rebelled against the materialistic interpretation of pragmatism characteristic of his own culture, but the Taoist text means no such thing.

7. Wilhelm's rendition of this passage is also murky, largely because of the use of a number of Buddhist terms that he did not understand. This was unfortunate for Jung, who in his meditative fantasies quite evidently did "fall into the elements of body and mind, where material and psychological illusions take charge." Although Jung admits that he never followed the directions of the *Golden Flower* (which may be just as well considering the quality of the translation), nevertheless it is tempting to speculate on what would have happened had there been an accurate version of the text available to him.

8. This passage is added to balance the foregoing warning about becoming deadened through malpractice; one should not become senseless, yet neither should one pursue objects. As ever, balance in the center is the keynote.

9. "Loose ends" tend to come up "for no apparent reason" in quietude because of heightened awareness and lowered inhibitions. Wilhelm translates "the realms of form and desire" (a Buddhist term) as "the world of illusory desires." Again this was unfortunate for Jung, who showed a marked inability to distinguish between the realm of form and the realm of desire. This tended to skew his interpretations of fantasies and led him to imagine that golden flower meditation is culture-bound in spite of his belief in universal archetypes.

10. People who enter into contemplative practices without this sort of theoretical preparation are easily deluded by unusual psychic experiences. Jung, himself a prime model of this, projected his imaginations on Taoism and thus believed that the teaching of the golden flower came from "abnormal psychic states." This false belief may be attributed partly to Wilhelm's inexpert translation of the text, but

it also seems to be due in large measure to Jung's own arbitrary ideas and personalistic interpretations.

VI. Authenticating Experiences of Turning the Light Around

1. Wilhelm mistranslates "cannot be undergone responsibly by people with small faculties and small capacities" as "one must not content oneself with small demands." The question of capacity is extremely important in the teaching and practice of Taoist alchemy. In his introduction to the text, Wilhelm asserts that "as far as the Chinese psyche is concerned, a completely assured method of attaining definite psychic experiences is available." If the expression "definite psychic experiences" is supposed to mean authentic realization of the golden flower awakening, this statement would seem absurd in the context of Buddhism and Taoism. A more accurate reading of the text would have clarified Wilhelm's confusion on this point; it is a matter not of "the Chinese psyche" in general, but of the faculties and capacities of the individual. Jung would also have done well to observe the warning of the text that "you cannot handle attainment with a careless or arrogant attitude," for the careless arrogance of his essays on the *Golden Flower* hindered him from a more serious and sober investigation of Taoism as much as did lack of resources.

2. Zhang Boduan (Chang Po-tuan), founder of the Southern School of Completely Real Taoism, wrote of a similar experience in his *Introduction to Alchemy:* "The pores are like after a bath, the bones and circulatory system are like when fast asleep, the vitality and spirit are like husband and wife in blissful embrace, the earthly and heavenly souls are like child and mother remembering their love."

3. "Myriad pipes are all silent" refers to a mental state of profound quietude; "the bright moon is in mid sky" refers to clear awareness within stillness. Both are common metaphors in Taoism and Chan Buddhism.

4. This passage refers to the refinement of sensory experience realized through the golden flower practice. The "filling of the body" with stored energy is said to be sufficient in itself to preserve health and well-being, even without physical exercise. "Red blood becoming milk" is a common Taoist symbol of the sublimation of passion.

5. The *Visualization Scripture* is a popular Pure Land Buddhist text, the *Guan Wuliangshou jing* (Scripture on visualization of infinite life). There are many examples of Taoists borrowing and reinterpreting Buddhist symbolism, some of them more plausible than others. The *Hui Ming Ching*, a small fragment of which is included in the Wilhelm/Baynes version of the *Golden Flower*, provides numerous instances of Chan Buddhist sayings borrowed by Taoist yogis and given esoteric interpretations in terms of Taoist energy work. "Higher good is like water" comes from the *Tao Te Ching*.

6. The Buddha on the terrace of enlightenment is the essence of one's own mind. The *Visualization Scripture* itself says, "When you see Buddha, you are seeing your own mind; for mind is Buddha, mind makes Buddha."

7. Wilhelm translates "the spirit enters into a state of openness" as "the gods are in the valley," giving the text a primitive polytheistic sound that is not there at all in the original. It was evidently on the basis of this sort of mistranslation that Jung came to the conclusion that the concepts of Chinese philosophy are, as he said, "never taken psychologically." Nothing could be further from the truth.

As a result of his misconception about the nature of Taoist practical philosophy, Jung thought that he himself was a pioneer in psychological interpretation; but since he did not understand the original Taoist concepts to begin with, his attempts to interpret them psychologically were based on his own imaginations and not on the real meanings of the ideas as they are understood by Taoists themselves.

8. "The empty room producing light" is an expression from the famous ancient Taoist classic *Chuang-tzu*. This is one of the quotations from that classic commonly used by practitioners of the Complete Reality school of Taoism, who found it a fit metaphor for one of their experiences in quiet meditation. Chan Buddhists tend to downplay the feelings of such experiences as remoteness, clarity, and suffusion with light, for two main reasons. One is that such experiences are just signals of something and not goals in themselves. The other is that the impression they nevertheless create on the mind can be so strong that "the spoils of war are lost through celebration."

9. The image of ascent is often used in Taoist literature. Sun Bu-er, one of the great female adepts of Completely Real Taoism, concluded her classic collection of poems with this verse on "flying":

> At the right time, just out of the valley
> You rise lightly into the spiritual firmament.
> The jade girl rides a blue phoenix,
> The gold boy offers a scarlet peach.
> One strums a brocade lute amidst the flowers,
> One plays jewel pipes under the moon.
> One day immortal and mortal are separated,
> And you coolly cross the ocean.

(from Immortal Sisters)

10. The Buddhist meditation manual known as *Small Stopping and Seeing* was mentioned earlier. This passage refers to a more complete manual by the same author known as *Great Stopping and Seeing*.

11. "When people drink water, they know for themselves whether it is cool or warm" is a common Chan Buddhist expression used to illustrate the fact that there is no way to communicate or understand realization of spiritual awakening except by one's own personal experience.

12. "A grain, and then another grain, from vagueness to clarity" is an often-quoted line from *Four Hundred Words on the Gold Elixir,* a short work by the founder of the Southern School of Completely Real Taoism, Zhang Boduan (Chang Po-tuan). Liu I-ming explains, "'Grain after grain' means that when the basis is established, the path develops and the positive energy gradually grows. It does not literally mean there is the form of grains" (*The Inner Teachings of Taoism*).

13. In his classic *Understanding Reality,* Chang Po-tuan also writes, "Truly it is said of a grain of the gold elixir that a snake that swallows it is immediately transformed into a dragon and a chicken that eats it is then changed into a phoenix, flying into the pure realm of true yang." Liu I-ming explains, "When yin and yang combine into one, the celestial order is clearly revealed; the innate knowledge and capacity which had been about to fade away in people is round and bright, clean and bare. A bead of gold elixir hangs in the center of vast space, lighting up the universe to view, unobstructed in all directions. When people ingest a grain of this elixir, they immediately become immortals."

VII. The Living Method of Turning the Light Around

A "living method" is one that is efficiently adapted to individual needs and integrated into everyday life. A "dead method" is one that is performed mechanically as an automatic routine. Chan Buddhist proverb says, "Study the living word, not the dead word."

1. "You need not give up your normal occupation." According to his own writing, Jung was of the opinion that yoga practice needs an ecclesiastical setting. Some professional Japanese Zennists also share this belief, and many Western Zennists following latter-day Japanese schools have therefore come to believe that Zen has traditionally been a primarily monastic movement. The fact that ecclesiastical operations generally call more attention to themselves than individual practitioners, who "hide their light" according to classical recommendations, has given Westerners the false impression that monasticism represented the mainstream of Eastern spiritual practice.

2. As the formless practice of turning the light around is repeated in the midst of everyday affairs, the mind becomes increasingly fluid and buoyant, able to engage in ordinary activities without getting stuck on things.

3. The keynote of this passage is "not sticking to any image of person or self at all." According to his own reports, Jung was fascinated by the images that came to mind when he tried to meditate according to his own method, which he apparently believed to be similar to that of the golden flower. Inasmuch as this sort of preoccupation is rigorously proscribed in Taoist meditation texts, it is no wonder at all

that Jung's work shows no indication that he really experienced anything like the golden flower awakening.

"If you can look back again and again into the source of mind, whatever you are doing" is rendered by Wilhelm as "When in ordinary life one has the ability always to react to things by reflexes only," which is not only technically incorrect but potentially dangerous. "Turning the light around wherever you are" is translated by Wilhelm as "circulation of the light arising out of circumstances." This small misreading of the words is greatly misleading if it means that the practice depends on circumstances.

4. Although the practice lacks power if it cannot be carried out in the midst of activity, it becomes easier if a quiet time is set aside early in the morning to refresh and orient the mind in turning the light around. "The realized ones in Heaven will surely come to attest to your experience" means that higher or more refined levels of awareness become accessible to consciousness, experientially proving the efficacy of the practice.

VIII. The Secret of Freedom

Wilhelm translates the title of this section as "A Magic Spell for the Far Journey." He tends to read weird and superstitious ideas into the text. Then again, it was not unusual for people of his time to expect Eastern ideas to be exotic and mysterious. The word translated as "magic spell" actually means a spoken teaching, or a secret teaching. It also comes to mean "secret" in the everyday how-to sense of what is essential for success in accomplishing something. As for "the far journey," this expression, which literally means "roaming" and really means "freedom of action," is the title of the opening chapter of *Chuang-tzu,* one of the most popular Taoist classics.

1. Jadelike purity is one of the "three purities," which are said to be realms of higher awareness to which Taoist adepts and immortals ascend. Thus they are representative of sources of inspiration for latter-day Taoist texts received through mediums in trance.

   According to Liu I-ming, "White snow symbolizes the energy of the primordial unity; this is like the metaphor of 'white light arising in the empty room.'" That this white snow flies in "midsummer" means that it is manifested in the "fire" of consciousness.

   The "sun blazing" symbolizes positive energy, "water" stands for real knowledge hidden within, and "midnight" represents profound stillness. Therefore "the sun blazing in the water at midnight" means the emergence of the positive energy of real knowledge from the depths of quietude.

   The receptive is the *I Ching* symbol for mother earth. Liu I-ming says, "If people can be flexible and yielding, humble, with self-control, entirely free of agitation, cleared of all volatility, not angered by criticism, ignoring insult, docilely accepting all hardships, illnesses, and natural disasters, utterly without anxiety or resentment when faced with danger or adversity, then people can be companions of earth" (*Awakening to the Tao*).

2. "The homeland of nothing whatsoever" is another expression from the Taoist classic *Chuang-tzu*. It appears at the end of the first chapter, "Freedom," after which this section of the *Golden Flower* text is named: in the ancient classic, the philosopher Chuang-tzu says, "Now you have a huge tree and worry that it is useless. Why don't you plant it in the vast plain of the homeland of Nothing Whatsoever, roaming in effortlessness by its side and sleeping in freedom beneath it? The reason it does not fall to the axe, and no one injures it, is that it cannot be used. So what's the trouble?"

3. "To act purposefully without striving" is translated by Wilhelm as "action through non-action." It is not certain what he meant by this. Wilhelm renders "indifferent emptiness" as "numbing emptiness," which could be right except for the impression it conveys that "emptiness" is itself "numbing." This expression should rather be rendered as "numb emptiness." Only "numb emptiness" is "numbing," not real emptiness as understood and experienced in Buddhism and Completely Real Taoism. Here again, acquaintance with Buddhist thought would have helped Wilhelm to understand the point of this passage.

4. The "center" is explained in the notes to paragraph 15 of Section III; the "two eyes" are explained in the notes to paragraph 4 of Section III. The "handle of the stars" refers to the crux or key of awareness, by which self-mastery and autonomy are attained.

5. The alchemical symbol of metal or lead is explained by Liu I-ming in his commentary on Chang Po-tuan's *Four Hundred Words on the Gold Elixir* in these terms: "Lead is dense and heavy, hard and strong, lasts long without disintegrating; what is called true lead here is not ordinary material lead, but is the formless, immaterial true sense of real knowledge in the human body. This true sense is outwardly dark but inwardly bright, strong and unbending, able to ward off external afflictions, able to stop internal aberrations. It is symbolized by lead and so is called the true lead. . . . Because its light illumines myriad existents, it is also called the golden flower. Because it is the pivot of creation, it is also called the North Star. Because it conceals light within darkness, it is also called metal within water" (*The Inner Teachings of Taoism*).

6. The "lower two passes" are the first two stages of a tradi-

tional formulation of Taoist spiritual alchemy: "refining vitality into energy," and "refining energy into spirit." The "upper pass" is the stage of "refining spirit into openness." At this point "Heaven directly divulges the unsurpassed doctrine" in the sense that knowledge comes spontaneously through elevation of consciousness rather than by formal learning.

7. The "outside" is surface consciousness, the "inside" is the "true sense of real knowledge" hidden below. To "control the inside from the outside" means to reach deliberately for this real knowledge and stabilize its connection with consciousness. To "control the outside from the inside" means to be rooted in real knowledge and thereby spontaneously control the activity of the conscious mind. The "master" is the true sense of real knowledge; the "assistant" is the conscious mind.

8. The *celestial mind* is a Taoist term for what Chan Buddhists call the *original mind*. This refers to the mind as it is in its pristine state unaffected by temporal conditioning.

9. This section of the text, particularly from this passage onward, is more thickly veiled than ever in the garb of Taoist alchemical language. Here the meaning becomes ambiguous in the sense that it can be interpreted in terms of the waterwheel exercise of Taoist energetics so popular in the Southern School of Complete Reality, or in purely spiritual terms characteristic of Chan Buddhism and the Northern School of Complete Reality Taoism. In terms of energetics, the "chamber of *water*" means the lower abdomen, where energy is built up for circulation. In spiritual terms, the "chamber of *water*" refers to the true sense of real knowledge hidden within temporal conditioning. I have italicized *water* because it stands for one of the main signs

of the *I Ching*, consisting of one solid (positive) line surrounded by two broken (negative) lines: in Taoist alchemy, this represents the primal hidden within the temporal.

10. The *I Ching* sign for *fire*, which represents consciousness, consists of two positive lines surrounding a negative line. In this case, the negative line represents temporal conditioning ruling consciousness. The sign for *the creative*, which represents the enlightened mind, consists of three positive lines. *Fire* is in substance *the creative* in the sense that consciousness is itself enlightenment; but this is not realized because of the influence of mundane conditioning.

11. "Negative energy stops" because the exercise of turning the light around vitiates the power of conditioned thought habits.

12. The joining of the positive energy in *water* and *the creative* means the reuniting of conscious knowledge and real knowledge. The "basic chamber" is the center, which again may be interpreted psychophysiologically or spiritually. Wilhelm renders "the positivity in *water*" as "the polarized light-line of the Abysmal," which is not very meaningful and certainly does not convey the sense of the positivity, creativity, or celestial nature of the "light" that the text emphasizes.

13. The movement of creative energy becomes "traceless" and "indiscernible" in the sense that the ecstasy accompanying the initial mating of consciousness and the true sense of real knowledge later subsides in favor of a more subtle experience.

14. "Living midnight" is a Taoist term for a state of profound mental stillness and quietude that is nevertheless pregnant with primal energy, preceding the "dawn" of resurgent

light. The restless "human mind" is stilled so that the clear "celestial mind" may come to light. Wilhelm translates "living midnight," which is an extremely common expression in this sort of Taoist literature, as "the time when the child comes to life."

15. The images of the master becoming a servant and taking the servant for the master are common in Chan Buddhism. In Taoist terms, this means that the mundane conditioning of the "human mentality" comes to govern the whole mind and is consequently mistaken for the self.

16. The *root of heaven* and *moon cavern* are alchemical terms for the movement of energy emerging from stillness and returning to stillness. They can also be expressed as the points of shift from passivity to activity and from activity to passivity.

17. In alchemical language, the positive creative energy of unconditioned primal awareness must be consciously "culled" or "gathered" when it emerges from the shrouds of unconsciousness. If it is not gathered, or if it is gathered too late, the positive energy is ineffective and mundane conditioning reasserts its power.

18. In Taoist energetics, "the chamber of *the creative*" is the head: energy is drawn by attention upward from the lower torso (the chamber of *water*) through the spine and into the head. In purely spiritual Taoism, the energy of the initial stirring of the "celestial mind" of unconditioned awareness is fostered until it becomes complete awakening, as symbolized by *the creative*. Focusing on the crown of the head is a method of enhancing alertness (to prevent quiet stillness from slipping into oblivion) and is only for temporary use at appropriate times.

19. In energetics, the "yellow court" is the middle of the body, where the energy is conducted after passing through the head. In spiritual practice, this means that heightened awareness is centered to keep the mind from floating off into utter abstraction.

20. In Chan Buddhism this experience is described in terms of "melting" or "unlocking" to indicate a transition from bondage to freedom.

21.–25. The six senses are the faculties of seeing, hearing, tasting, smelling, feeling, and thinking. Not using the six senses is believed to be the most excellent form of hygiene, both mental and physical, practiced by Taoists to restore and preserve spirit and energy. Paragraphs 21 to 23 describe three levels of profundity in experience of the same exercise; paragraph 25 illustrates their interpenetration. This scheme of three stages, each also containing three, or a total of nine, stages, derives from the teaching of the ninth-century Chan master Linji, who was regarded as the founder of virtually all the lines of Chan Buddhism extant at the time of the writing of *The Secret of the Golden Flower*.

26. The three and nine stages are spoken of in relation to the subjective experience of the practitioner, but all are objectively of the same source. The "interval of a world cycle" means the interval between stirring of mind and return to quiescence.

27. "Action caused by momentum is random action, not essential action." This means that one should learn to act objectively, first quieting the mind so as to be able to act from a state of cool clarity rather than by impulse. Wilhelm translates, "One moves the movement and forgets the move-

ment; this is not movement in itself." It is not clear what he thought this might have meant.

28. "This does not contrast the action of Heaven to the nature of Heaven" in that it does not consider stillness superior to action; both action and stillness are part of the total enlightenment as long as they proceed from the primal unconditioned source of mind rather than from temporal habit.

29. Desire as considering things to exist or desire as being possessive toward things are typically Buddhist definitions. Desire as thought that is out of place and based on ulterior motives is a typical neo-Confucian definition.

30. Wilhelm translates "spontaneous attention" as "a movement without purpose," and "acting without striving" as "action through non-action." Neither of these expressions hits the mark, but from the point of view of cross-cultural studies it is significant to take note of them as reflections of standard misconceptions of Eastern mysticism.

31. In paragraph 10 of this section, the yin line inside the symbol of *fire* is understood as "false yin," which means mundane conditioning. Here it is understood as "true yin," which means calmness. The operation referred to as "taking from *water* to fill in *fire*" consists of replacing the negative line (temporal conditioning) inside *fire* (consciousness) with the positive line (real knowledge) inside *water* (the depths of the unconscious). This formula comes from the alchemical classic *Understanding Reality*, which says, "Take the solid in the heart of the position of *water*, and change the yin in the innards of the palace of *fire*. From this transformation comes the sound body of *heaven* (*the creative*) — to lie hidden or to fly and leap is all up to the mind." Liu I-ming

explains, "The solid in the heart of the position of *water* is the real knowledge in the mind of Tao; the yin in the innards of the palace of *fire* is the conscious knowledge of the human mind. Take out the reality-knowing mind of Tao that has fallen into water and with it replace the consciously knowing mind in the palace of fire. In a short time the yin (temporal) energy will dissolve and the yang (primal) energy will return, and you will again see the original face of *heaven*, recovering your original nature of innate knowledge and innate capacity, tranquil and unperturbed yet sensitive and effective, sensitive and effective yet tranquil and undisturbed."

32. The "breeze of *wind*" symbolizes gradual penetration through following an initiatory process. Here it means the use of focused consciousness to gain access to real knowledge hidden in the unconscious.

33. "Nurturing the fire" means developing consciousness by calm and flexible receptivity.

34. *Bathing* is also a key alchemical term. According to *The Book of Balance and Harmony*, in the higher type of gradual method "bathing" means "being suffused with harmonious energy," while in the very highest type of alchemy it means "cleaning the mind."

35. The expression "stopping at ultimate good" comes from the ancient Confucian classic *Daxue* (*Ta Hsueh*; The Great Learning) and is commonly employed in later Taoist alchemical texts. "The infinite" is a Taoist and neo-Confucian term for the state of awareness prior to discursive discrimination.

36. "Activating the mind without dwelling on anything" is a famous line from the popular Buddhist *Diamond Cutter Scripture*. The sixth patriarch of Chan Buddhism is said to

have become enlightened on hearing this line of scripture being recited as he was passing through a marketplace.

As for "effecting openness," *The Book of Balance and Harmony* says, "Taoism, Buddhism, Confucianism—all simply transmit one openness. Throughout all time, those who have transcended have done the work from within openness. Openness and sincerity are the essence of alchemy, learning Buddhism is meditation plunging into openness; and as for learning the affairs of Confucian sages, selflessness in openness clarifies the celestial design."

37. Again Wilhelm proposes a misleading translation: "to be unminding in all situations" he renders as "forever dwelling in purposelessness." It is likely that Jung derived some of his more bizarre ideas about Eastern philosophy from just such mistranslations as this one. In the beginning of Section VI it says that in order to develop the capacity to undergo the experience of the golden flower awakening responsibly it is necessary to will the liberation of all beings; so the very idea of "purposelessness" is incompatible with this practice. Although Wilhelm translates that part somewhat clumsily, nevertheless the meaning does come through there; apparently it slipped his mind when he came to this section. The term *wuxin* (unminding) is a common Chan Buddhist expression.

38. "Contemplating emptiness, the conditional, and the center" is a fundamental meditative exercise of Tiantai (T'ien-t'ai) Buddhism. Again Wilhelm shows virtually complete ignorance of Buddhism in any context but standard Western cliché, translating "the conditional" as "delusion." In reality, the conditional per se is not delusion; delusion means to mistake the conditional for a fixed or independent reality in itself.

39.–43. Paragraphs 39 to 43 present what may be the simplest and most concise statement of this Tiantai Buddhist practice to be found anywhere: the point is to achieve a state of centered mental poise wherein both the fluidity and factuality of phenomena are evident to the mind without either exerting an overwhelming influence toward bias.

According to this way of meditation, by realization of fluidity the mind transcends attachment to conditional things; by realization of factuality the mind transcends attachment to emptiness. By realization of the center, one attains a harmonious unity of freedom and responsibility. In Tiantai Buddhism the accomplishment of this practice is called "three insights in one mind."

44. *Fire* is spirit, *water* is vitality. Alchemists sometimes say that Buddhism starts with *fire* while Taoism starts with *water.*

45. Here "the two eyes" is meant literally. There is a strong tendency to place great emphasis on the data of sight in everyday life, so the text makes it clear that all the faculties of sense and perception are channels of enlightened awareness. The third patriarch of Chan Buddhism wrote, "The six senses aren't bad, they are the same as true awakening."

46. This means that the true sense of real knowledge, which in ordinary people falls into abeyance in the unconscious, must be "resurrected" by consciousness through the exercise of deliberate attention.

47. The darkness in the sun is true yin within true yang, flexibility within firmness.

48. The white of the moon is true yang within true yin, firmness within flexibility.

49. A verse in the alchemical classic *Understanding Reality* says,

"The sun, in the position of *fire*, turns into a woman; *water*, in the moon palace, turns out to be a man."

IX. Setting Up the Foundation in a Hundred Days

This and the following three sections, comprising the rest of the text as it is found in the canonical version on which the present translation is based, are entirely omitted by Wilhelm in his rendition, because he considers them of "inferior quality." He does not explain, however, the basis of this evaluation. While it is true that these last four chapters go back to basics again and again, this is in fact a general characteristic of the whole text, which repeatedly reviews fundamental theory and praxis as it develops the details of their experiential implications. It may be that the difficulty of these sections, which contain relatively high concentrations of Buddhist and Taoist technical terms, discouraged Wilhelm from attempting to translate them.

1. There are a number of scriptures with the generic *Mind Seal* title in the Taoist canon. The practice of one hundred days setting up the foundation to stabilize consciousness is common in Taoist alchemy. Here when the text says "you are still working with the light of the eyes," this means that at the outset a practitioner is using ordinary consciousness, not the refined consciousness referred to by the terms "spirit," "essence," and "wisdom."

2. "Intercourse" and "formation of the embryo" are standard alchemical images. Chang Po-tuan's classic *Four Hundred Words on the Gold Elixir* says, "When husband and wife mate, clouds and rain form in the secret room. In a year

they give birth to a child, and each rides on a crane." Liu I-ming explains, "Our real knowledge is yang within yin; this is the 'husband.' Our conscious knowledge is yin within yang; this is the 'wife.' After the primal yang in people culminates, acquired conditioning takes over affairs, and the real gets lost outside, as though it lived in another house and did not belong to oneself. Though one may have conscious knowledge, the wife does not see the husband; yin being without the balance of yang, this consciousness has falsehood in it. If the husband, real knowledge, is recognized and called back home to meet the wife, conscious knowledge, and taken into the privacy of the secret room, the husband loves the wife and the wife loves the husband; husband and wife mate, sense and essence combine, so the primal energy comes forth from within nothingness and congeals into the spiritual embryo" (*The Inner Teachings of Taoism*).

When the text says that "if you entertain any conceptual view at all, this is immediately a misleading path," this means that conceptual views are products of the temporally conditioned consciousness and thus deviate attention from the primal essence of consciousness. Chan Buddhism is well known for insistence on detachment from conceptual views in order to "perceive essence and attain Buddhahood."

3. Generally speaking, references to points or periods of time in alchemical literature refer not to clock or calendar time but to psychological time. Intense condensation of experiential time is also characteristic of mental concentration in the alchemical process. In his classic *Understanding Reality*, Chang Po-tuan writes, "Changing hours for days is the pattern of the spiritual work." Liu I-ming explains, "Developed people, emulating the image of the sun and moon

meeting, place thirty days within one day, and also place one day within one hour: in one hour activating strong energy, they use the human mind to produce the mind of Tao, use the mind of Tao to govern the human mind, produce real knowledge by conscious knowledge, and purge conscious knowledge by real knowledge; they gather the undifferentiated primal energy for the mother of the elixir, and follow the spiritual mechanism of the transformations of yin and yang as the firing process."

4. Empowerment refers to the stabilization of the higher consciousness so that one can turn the light around at will in any and all circumstances. This may require a period of special effort, represented by the hundred days setting up the foundation.

5. In both Chan Buddhism and the Northern School of Completely Real Taoism, "seeing essence," directly experiencing the essence of consciousness in itself, is temporarily set up as an aim for those who are bound up in the products of consciousness and thereby alienated from its essence. After "seeing essence" is attained, it then becomes a means rather than an end: a means of freeing mental energy for further development. Because "seeing essence" can give a false sense of confidence before the union of conscious knowledge and real knowledge is matured, enlightened guidance is needed. The classical statement of this principle in Chan Buddhism says, "First awaken on your own, then see someone else." Here the text says "everything that emerges naturally from essence is tested" in the sense that it is necessary to examine the subsequent activity of consciousness for remaining taints of compulsive mental habit ruled by mundane conditioning. This is one of the most important functions of a guide.

X. The Light of Essence and
the Light of Consciousness

The distinction between "the light of essence" and "the light of consciousness" is critical to success in the practice of Taoist alchemy or Chan Buddhism. Paragraph 1 in Section II makes this clear when it says, "Only the true essence of the original spirit transcends the primal organization and is above it."

It is unfortunate that Wilhelm did not translate this tenth section, because if properly understood it would have been of inestimable value to Jung, who was evidently unable to make the critical distinction in his own experience. Indeed, Jung does not seem to have even had a clear theoretical grasp of this issue; what he assigns to the "unconscious" would in Taoism still be considered part of the consciousness of the human mentality, not the essence that "transcends the primal organization."

An often-quoted classic verse on this subject by the great ninth-century Chan master Changsha clearly defines the central importance of the distinction between the "light of consciousness" and the "light of essence" in these terms: "When people who study the Way do not know reality, it is just because they have been giving their recognition to the conscious spirit all along: this is the root of beginningless eons of birth and death, yet fools call it the original being." From the point of view of the traditions of Chan Buddhism and Completely Real Taoism, Jung's confusion on this point is evident throughout his commentary on the *Golden Flower* and other texts from Asian spiritual teachings.

1. In modern times, followers of sectarian Zen and Taoism have come to lay great stress on sitting meditation, but classical masters have pointed out that addiction to stillness can have serious mental and physical drawbacks. If the practice of "turning the light around" is carried on only in specific

settings or postures, it may be impossible to integrate it fully with everyday life, leading to a kind of split in the personality.

2. This passage makes it clear that the "light" of essence has nothing to do with visionary experiences. *Boshan Canchan Jingce,* a well-known Chan meditation manual dating from about a century before the *Golden Flower* text, says, "If you see lights, flowers, or other extraordinary forms, and take this for sanctity, using these unusual phenomena to dazzle people, thinking you have attained great enlightenment, you do not realize that you are thoroughly ill. This is not Chan."

3. The mirror being "occupied" by an image represents the attention being occupied by the contents of consciousness and thus losing sight of the essence of consciousness. This is also a good description of what happened to Jung when he tried to meditate and became mired in images arising from his subconscious.

4. The Yellow Emperor (Huang Di) is one of the major figures of antiquity associated both with Taoism and with the founding of proto-Chinese culture. The "echoes" here symbolize the thoughts or contents of consciousness; to say they are "not sound" means that thoughts are not themselves the essence of consciousness, even though they arise from the movement of consciousness.

5. The *Heroic March Scripture* (*Surangama-sutra*) is a Buddhist text that became particularly popular among Chan Buddhist contemplatives from the Sung dynasty (960–1278) onward. The following passages of the *Golden Flower* text, paragraphs 5 to 10, briefly outline a meditation exercise from that scripture, known as the "eight attributions,"

which is designed to facilitate "perception of essence" through a sort of process of elimination. The eight attributions are usually defined as follows:

1. Light is attributable to the sun.
2. Dark is attributable to the dark moon.
3. Transmission is attributable to doors and windows.
4. Obstruction is attributable to walls.
5. Objects are attributable to discrimination.
6. Blank openness is attributable to space.
7. Congestion is attributable to sense data.
8. Clear light is attributable to clarity.

By gradually "peeling away" the contents of consciousness, the practitioner ultimately reaches the experience of the essence of consciousness.

10. The *eighth consciousness* is a Buddhist term: it is also called the *storehouse consciousness*. One aspect of the storehouse consciousness is its function as the repository of impressions. This is close to what Jung calls the "unconscious," but Jung differs from Buddhism in considering the unconscious a basic reality. Another aspect of the storehouse consciousness, which comes out after it has been clarified, is its function of "mirrorlike awareness." This is a basic experience of Buddhist transformation of consciousness, but it is not final. In dealing with both aspects of the eighth consciousness, Buddhist practice aims at "smashing through" it and removing fixation even on these levels of experience. Chan and Zen Buddhist literature suggest that Jung was most definitely not alone in getting bogged down in the eighth consciousness. Unlike the Chan and Zen Buddhists, however, Jung was not fortunate enough to have authentic technical literature sufficient to diagnose the problem.

11. Sometimes the exercise of turning the light around is described as looking to see where thought comes from, but this is not the same as the psychoanalytic exercise of looking to see the unconscious roots of conscious manifestations. In Chan practice, psychoanalysis comes *after* "seeing essence," because it is only from the central standpoint of essence that the contents of consciousness can be witnessed objectively.

12. "Flow and revolve" is a Buddhist expression for routine mental habit. The final passages of this section return to the critical distinction between the "flowing and revolving" consciousness and the transcendental essence. This paragraph makes it clear that even "emptiness," when experienced as an item of the conscious inventory, is still just an object, not the open essence of mind. Mistaking a feeling or state of "emptiness" for emptiness itself is a psychological phenomenon often mentioned in Zen classics.

XI. The Intercourse of *Water* and *Fire*

1. Here *fire* stands for conscious knowledge and *water* stands for real knowledge. The intercourse of *water* and *fire* represents the union of the real knowledge of the mind of Tao and the conscious knowledge of the human mind.

2. The yin inside *fire* stands for receptivity, and also for mundane conditioning. The yang inside *water* stands for the firmness of the true sense of real knowledge.

3. In his explanation of Chang Po-tuan's *Four Hundred Words on the Gold Elixir*, Liu I-ming says, "If you understand that the foundation of water and fire of real knowledge and conscious knowledge originally belong to one energy, and if

you cultivate them backward, inverting water and fire, using real knowledge to control conscious knowledge, using conscious knowledge to nurture real knowledge, water and fire balance each other, movement and stillness are as one; then mind is Tao, Tao is mind" (*The Inner Teachings of Taoism*).

XII. The Cycle

1. The Southern School of Taoism tends to value the water-wheel exercise, wherein a mass of energy is developed and circulated throughout the body. When the *Golden Flower* text says "energy is not the main thing," this is an indication of its roots in the Northern School under Chan Buddhist influence.

2. *The Book of Balance and Harmony* says, "The North Star, never shifting, governs motion." It also says, "The North Star is the heart of heaven and earth," and "When the human mind is calm and quiet, like the North Star not shifting, the spirit is most open and aware. For one who sees this, the celestial Tao is within oneself."

3. "Culling" is just a metaphor; *The Book of Balance and Harmony* says, "The medicinal ingredients are just culled in nonbeing."

4. "Indulgence" is a Buddhist term for what Taoists call "leaking," or the expenditure of conscious energy in pursuit of objects.

5. Dragon and tiger, water and fire, are metaphors for yin and yang. The meaning of this passage is not entirely clear, but it seems to refer to dilettantism.

6. There are times of interaction and noninteraction of real knowledge and conscious knowledge as long as their union has not been stabilized.

7. A poem entitled "Combining Yin and Yang" in *The Book of Balance and Harmony* says, "To reach the Tao is basically not hard; the work lies in concentration. When yin and yang, above and below, always rise and descend, the ubiquitous flow of vital sense naturally returns of itself. At the peak of awareness, reality becomes accessible to consciousness; in recondite abstraction, nondoing joins with doing. When the clouds recede and the rain disperses, the spiritual embryo is complete; the creative principle comes into play, producing a new birth."

8. Definitions of process and cycle are matters of method; at this point the means are transcended and there is no conscious fixation on expedient distinctions. According to Buddhist metaphor, this is like "leaving the raft behind on reaching the other shore."

9. This passage reiterates the fundamental continuity of the individual and the universe, the identity of mind and the world it experiences. The third patriarch of Chan Buddhism wrote in his famous *Poem on Trusting Mind*, "There is nowhere it is not; the ten directions are right before the eyes. Most minute, it is the same as the great; you forget all about objects. Most great, it is the same as the minute; you do not see any outside." A proverb common in both Chan and Taoist literature says, "It is so great that there is nothing outside it, so small it enters where there is no space." Chang Po-tuan's alchemical classic *Understanding Reality* also says, "The essence of the self enters the essence of the

enlightened; the essence of enlightenment is everywhere thus. From on high the cold light shines in the cold springs; one moon appears in a thousand ponds. Its smallness is smaller than a hair, its greatness fills the universe."

10. Spontaneity is the real meaning of the Taoist technical term *wuwei*, often mistranslated by Wilhelm and others as "non-action" or "inaction." The Taoist classic *Huainanzi* (The masters of Huainan), explains spontaneity in these terms: "Real people know without learning, see without looking, achieve without striving, understand without trying. They sense and respond, act when necessary, go when there is no choice, like the shining of light, like the emanation of rays."

11. "Clouds forming and rain falling" is a standard metaphor deriving from the ancient classic *I Ching*. It represents the harmonious combination of yin and yang producing living energy.

12. "Living midnight" is explained in the notes to paragraph 14 of Section VIII. The term "true midnight" is relatively rare in alchemical literature, as compared to "living midnight." It is sometimes taken literally to mean the middle of the night, as a time of external quiet suitable for fostering internal stillness. Metaphorically, it stands for extreme tranquillity; it is distinguished from "living midnight" in that the latter expression emphasizes the subtle presence of potential and the imminent awakening of positive energy.

13. *Understanding Reality* says, "Real enlightenment has no likeness; a single round light engulfs myriad forms. The bodiless body is the real body; the formless form is the real form."

14. Here it would seem that "midnight" is used as an equivalent to the Buddhist term "emptiness," which is experienced right in the midst of forms.

15. Following the Buddhist pattern, to "head for the true" means to cultivate perception of emptiness in the conditional; "the living" then corresponds to the conditional in emptiness.

XIII. Song to Inspire the World

0. "Cinnabar heart" has a dual meaning. The word for cinnabar is also used for the color of cinnabar. The color of cinnabar is in the family of red, which is the color of compassion in Buddhism. This is the external meaning, which would probably be obvious in context even without knowledge of this traditional association. In chemical terms, cinnabar contains mercury. In alchemical terms, mercury symbolizes the mercurial nature of consciousness, so cinnabar symbolizes the matrix of consciousness.

   Many of the expressions and ideas used in the verses of the following song have already appeared in the text, some of them more than once. There are a few, however, that are new or call for further comment in this context:

1. By poise in the center it is possible to bear change as it pervades all conditioned things.

2. The "mysterious pass" is defined by *The Book of Balance and Harmony* in these terms: "Sages just used the word 'center' to point out the opening of the mysterious pass. This 'center' is it. Let me give you a convenient simile. When a puppet moves its hands and feet and gesticulates in a hundred ways, it is not that the puppet can move. It is moved by pulling strings. And though it is a string device, it is the person controlling the puppet who pulls the strings. Do you know this person who controls the puppet? The puppet is like the body, the strings are like the mysterious pass;

the person controlling the puppet is like the innermost self. The movements of the body are not done by the body; it is the mysterious pass that makes it move. But though it is the action of the mysterious pass, still it is the innermost self that activates the mysterious pass. If you can recognize this activating mechanism, without a doubt you can become a wizard."

3. Midnight stands for the moment of transition from rest to activity; noon stands for the moment of transition from activity to rest. The whole line means "all the time," but special attention is called to the transitions represented by midnight and noon, which occur not only from day to day but also from hour to hour in action and rest and from moment to moment in thought.

4. The "primal opening" is described by Chang Po-tuan in his *Four Hundred Words on the Gold Elixir* in these terms: "This opening is not an ordinary aperture: made by heaven and earth together, it is called the lair of spirit and energy" (*The Inner Teachings of Taoism*).

5. The "river source that produces the medicine" is an image from Chang Po-tuan's *Understanding Reality*, which says, "If you want to know the location of the river source which produces the herb, it is just in the southwest, its original homeland." Liu I-ming explains, "The southwest is the direction of *earth*, the realm where the new moon returns, where yin at its extreme gives birth to yang. In people, this is the time of beginning movement when stillness has reached its extreme. This movement from the extreme of stillness is precisely when the great medicine appears. However, this movement is not the stirring of emotions at external influences, and it is not the stirring of thoughts in the

mind. It is the movement of the innate knowledge of the natural mind, the movement of the real knowledge of the mind of Tao."

8.–9. In psychophysiological Taoist energetics, *water* is associated with the genitals, *fire* is associated with the heart: the intercourse of water and fire is then defined as placing the attention (associated with the heart) in the lower abdomen (associated with the genitals). According to *The Book of Balance and Harmony*, this practice is in the lower grade of gradual methods. The attitude toward this practice expressed here by *The Doctrine of the Golden Flower* is another typical indication of its purism.

16. The "water-clarifying pearl" is a Buddhist metaphor for enlightenment, or for the pure mind.

18. The "jade capital" is a Taoist symbol for the supreme spiritual state. Nine is the number for yang, symbolizing positive energy in full bloom; dragons represent the inconceivable fluidity of spirit.

20. In the terminology of *I Ching* symbolism as it is used in Taoist alchemy, *wind* stands for accord and penetration; lightning is associated with *fire*, which stands for awareness and understanding. Together they form the sign called *The Cauldron*, which represents "producing illumination through following an initiatory process," according to Liu I-ming's explanation in *The Taoist I Ching*. The symbol of *thunder* is movement, specifically the initial activation of positive energy in the sense of real knowledge.

21. Here again it is made clear that the opening of the enhanced consciousness known as the golden flower is not a matter of routine performance of yogic exercises.

The image of "retreating to hide in secrecy" is explained in *The Book of Balance and Harmony* in these terms: "It is written, 'The sages used the Changes [the *I Ching*] to clean their hearts, and withdrew into recondite secrecy.' What does this mean? It is the consummation of sincerity and truthfulness. The principles of the Changes extend throughout the macrocosm and the microcosm; sages ponder the principles of the Changes to clean their hearts and thoughts, and store them in ultimate sincerity."

22. The two poems used by Lu Yan when initiating Zhang Zhennu, who was to become a famous Immortal Sister, a female Taoist adept, are quoted with an energetics-oriented interpretation in *Spiritual Alchemy for Women*. The original verses read,

> After midnight and before noon,
> Settle the breathing and sit.
> As the energy goes through
> The double pass at midspine
> And on through the brain,
> Gaining the power of energy
> Contemplate the self.
>
> You must find the ancestor of your own house.
> Thunder in the earth rumbles,
> Setting in motion rain on the mountain.
> Wait until washing,
> And the yellow sprouts emerge from earth.
> Grab the golden essence of vitality
> And lock it up tightly.
> Fire metal and wood
> To produce the dragon and tiger.
>
> (*Immortal Sisters*)

Translator's Afterword:

Modern Applications of the Golden Flower Method

For me the experience symbolized by the golden flower has always been a practical concern. This new translation of *The Secret of the Golden Flower* arose from a confluence of several courses of events. One of them was my own introduction to the golden flower practice of "turning the light around," long before I knew of the existence of this particular book. Finding that method of mindfulness extremely powerful and versatile, I subsequently spent many years studying its use in experience and looking for tested information pertaining to its objective application.

Eventually this pursuit led to studies of classical sourcebooks in Chinese, Sanskrit, and Japanese. I began translating relevant texts from Buddhist and Taoist traditions, because I felt that their psychological insights could be useful in some way to people today, wherever they were. Although I had not read his views on the subject, I agreed with Jung that such information should not be cloistered. Whoever we may be and whatever we may do, mind is at the heart of our lives; so the clarification and awakening of mind is of potential interest to everyone, in whatever walk of life.

131

For many years I focused on the study of Chan Buddhism, the Chinese precursor of Zen. Classical Chan appealed to me because it cut directly through to the essence of mind without being burdened by dogmatism or cultural accretions.

One of the most interesting ways this is done in Chan classics is by concentrating the teachings of the scriptures and schools of Buddhism into symbolic stories representing the underlying state of mind. Many of these stories are specifically for turning the light around, and because of my early experiences I was particularly interested in them. The more difficult and complex Chan stories dealing with creative integration of the golden flower mind with the ordinary world required mental work in everyday life and took much longer to begin to penetrate.

Eventually I learned to practice turning the light around according to the methods of all the major schools of Buddhism. At first I was most dramatically affected by the Chan and Pure Land ways of awakening this consciousness, but I subsequently found that the techniques of each school had their own advantages; so I continued to apply whatever worked best whenever I had a special quest and wanted renewed inspiration.

At the same time, I studied the various support systems devised by the schools to enable people to experience the golden flower consciousness in meaningful ways. I found that this helped to clarify both practical and theoretical issues: what I was experiencing in everyday life and what I was finding in my researches in ancient Eastern literature on mind studies.

It was in connection with this course of events that I came into contact with Taoism. In the years following my first exposure to Buddhist teachings, I looked into other Asian classical traditions such as Hinduism, Confucianism, Taoism, and Sufism. I also read from the Bible, the Koran, and the mystic traditions of Judaism and Christianity. During these studies I found that turning the light around revealed unsuspected dimensions in the literature of other religions. A transcultural, transdogmatic appreciation of the mental dynamic of religion became manifest in a very direct manner by means of this technique.

My studies of world religions took place in several phases. The first phase of study was partly comparative, observing what was common to different religions and what was peculiar to each. This helped to distinguish local historical and cultural elements of religious presentations from perennial underlying concerns. I returned to these studies later, in connection with programs from the classical Pure Land, Zen, and Flower Ornament schools of Buddhism, each of which include investigation of other religions and philosophies as part of Buddhist study.

It was through the last phase of intertraditional study, as part of the practice of the comprehensive Flower Ornament school of Buddhism, that I returned to the study of Taoism. This new phase of research into Taoism focused heavily on inner alchemy, the processes of refining the mind and body as a unit joined by will. This eventually led me to *The Secret of the Golden Flower*, which combines Taoist alchemy with basic mind work according to the designs of several schools of Buddhism.

Over the years I had attempted to read the Wilhelm/Baynes translation of this important text several times, but found it inaccessible. Jung's commentary, moreover, seemed contradictory and confused. Giving up in frustration, I finally began to look for the original Chinese work.

It proved possible to find a good text in a condensed collection of essential works from the Taoist canon, along with an authentic commentary on the practical application of the teaching. By this time I had also read and translated other Buddhist and Taoist classics in the ancestral traditions of *The Secret of the Golden Flower* and therefore had become familiar with the technical terminology of the text.

The main difficulty of the original work is that it uses Taoist alchemical language mixed with several types of Buddhist Chinese. This undoubtedly caused Wilhelm confusion, because there were no facilities for teaching these languages and symbol systems to Westerners at that time. On comparison with the canonical version of the original Chinese text, it became clear that Wilhelm had misconstrued the text on many points, and his translation was unreliable.

There are enough flaws in Wilhelm's readings of grammar, terminology, and conceptual structures to render his translation practically dysfunctional. Perhaps sensing this, but attributing it to cultural differences, Jung went further afield in transmogrifying the central concepts of the text.

Jung warned his readers away from trying to practice the secret of the golden flower, professing psychoanalysis to be its Western equivalent. His reasoning was that

Europeans lacked the cultural basis for practicing Eastern disciplines and had to work with their own traditions. There is obviously some truth to this part of the argument, and Buddhists have long said that teachings must be adapted to local psychological and social climates. I do not agree, however, that Jung's approach to the unconscious outlined in his introduction to *The Secret of the Golden Flower* is actually equivalent to the golden flower practice.

What Jung seems to have been against in reality was blind imitation of techniques, undertaken with the wrong motivations and attitudes. This is a useful warning, and he himself was aware that Buddhist proverb says the same thing. It is not necessary to believe, however, that all Westerners will inevitably behave in this manner toward Eastern teachings. Furthermore, the behavior will not necessarily change simply because its object is changed. The problem is in the behavior, not in the object.

Jung's case against Westerners trying to practice the golden flower method would have been stronger if he had been able to clarify what was culture specific and could not be imitated usefully, and if he had adequately defined cultic behaviors that inhibit the efficiency of mind-purifying practices. But even so, he made a useful contribution to the study of this issue by raising doubts that needed expression and questions that called for examination.

Many Westerners today have had more opportunity for exposure to Eastern teachings and to psychological studies of cultism than had Jung and his contemporaries. Cult behavior continues to exist, nevertheless, so it is important to distinguish it from authentic spiritual practice. In order to do this, it is necessary to observe the cult mentality from the point of view of the golden flower and avoid confusing this process with observing the golden flower practice from the point of view of the cult mentality.

Jung's goal of understanding religion in terms of psychology was an approach that made religious teachings of all kinds more accessible to Westerners. Its full realization may have been thwarted by a combination of factors, including lack of sufficient data, due to which Jung was unable to understand Eastern teachings clearly and therefore could not come to definitive conclusions. Unaware that Taoists and Buddhists had themselves been interpreting religion psychologically for centuries, Jung was unable to avail himself of their methods.

The psychological approach to the study of religion is not itself invalidated, however, by the shortcomings in Jung's own practical work on Eastern teachings; on the contrary, it increases its validity with fuller and more accurate information and analysis. Jung's caveats about practice, therefore, should be understood in reference to cultism, which involves fixation and therefore cannot in any case foster authentic realization of golden flower mind blossoming.

In his time Jung did not have access to materials that would have allowed him to make distinctions between normal and cultic practices of Eastern teachings, and he could not objectively judge the relative merits of the different exercises found in the corrupted version of *The Secret of the Golden Flower* rendered by Wilhelm.

Furthermore, from sources such as Jung's introduction to the second German edition of *The Secret of the Golden Flower*, and works such as *Siddhartha* and *Magister Ludi* by Jung's contemporary Hermann Hesse, it is evident that fragmentary imitation Eastern mystical cults were thriving in Europe between the first and second world wars. Jung's reservations about golden flower practice were as much held in reaction to events in his own cultural milieu as they were based on his impressions of the text itself.

This fact seemed particularly significant to me, particularly insofar as one of the factors involved in my own long-standing interest in Chan and Zen Buddhism was the practice of transcending religious and cultural forms to get at the heart of reality in itself by direct experience and direct perception. While it is true that there are ritualized Zen cults with highly cloistered and involuted attitudes, these are generally examples of imitations described long ago in the classics of Chan and Zen, and as such they do not impugn the validity of the original teachings themselves.

Cultism, scholasticism, and cultural traditionalism aside, I believe that the essence of Chan is one of the most potentially useful elements of the golden flower teaching, and of Buddhism in general, in the context of the modern West. In addition to its psychoactive techniques, the psychological and intellectual structures of Chan lore can be superlative analytic tools that enable the mind to distinguish the inner patterns of things. Of course, their ultimate value in practice depends upon how effectively they are employed, as in their application to *The Secret of the Golden Flower.*

The theory and practice of the golden flower method do exist in Greek and Christian tradition, but if they are to be usefully analyzed in secular psychological terms, without an abundance of philosophical or religious concepts, I believe this can be most easily accomplished by means of Chan devices that require no background in Chinese culture to understand or employ.

The Secret of the Golden Flower represents a way of approaching completeness of energy through completeness of mind. This teaching calls itself a "special transmission outside of doctrine," free from attachment to dogma and form, based on direct perception of the essence of mind and recovery of its inherent potential. This is the hallmark of Chan, which is sometimes called the school of the enlightened mind.

For practical purposes, a distinction is made in the golden flower teaching between the "original spirit" and the "conscious spirit." The original spirit is the formless essence of awareness; it is unconditioned and transcends culture and history. The conscious spirit is the mind-set of feelings, thoughts, and attitudes, conditioned by personal and cultural history, bound by habit to specific forms. These terms are employed in both Chan and Taoist traditions.

Intuition belongs to the original spirit; intellect belongs to the conscious spirit. The essence of Taoism is to refine the conscious spirit to reunite it with the original spirit. In Chan Buddhism, the primal original spirit is also known as the host, while the conditioned conscious spirit is known as the guest; the original spirit is the master, and the conscious spirit is the servant. In these terms, self-delusion occurs when the servant has taken over from the master; self-enlightenment takes place when the master is restored to autonomy in the center.

The idea of two minds or two aspects of mind is found early on in the ancient Taoist classic *Tao Te Ching*: "Using the shining radiance, you return again to the light, not leaving anything to harm yourself. This is called entering the eternal." Here is an image of an ideal relationship between the original spirit as the source of power and the conscious spirit as a subordinate functionary. When clarified, the conscious spirit functions according to the situation without usurping the authority of the original spirit. The original spirit remains available as the reserve of total awareness, to which the conscious spirit returns without leaving any harmful fixation on itself or its objects.

In this way the intellect functions efficiently in the world without that conscious activity inhibiting access to deeper spontaneous knowledge through the direct intuition of a more subtle faculty.

The operation of switching from the limited mind of conditioned consciousness to the liberated mind of primal spirit is known as the method of "reversal," or turning around the light. In *The Secret of the Golden Flower* these terms refer to restoration of direct contact with the essence and source of awareness.

This direct contact empowers the individual to know spontaneously and be free from bondage to created thoughts and conditioned feelings, even while operating in their very presence. In the words of the *Tao Te Ching*, one can thus be "creative without possessiveness."

In both Taoism and Buddhism, the term *turning the light around* means turning the primary attention from involvement in mental objects to focus on the essence or source of mind. This exercise is practiced as a means of clearing consciousness and freeing awareness.

Many of the Taoists who had the strongest affinities with Chan Buddhism relied heavily on the exercise of turning the light around. Although this exercise is found in all Buddhist schools, it was particularly emphasized in Chan Buddhism. *The Secret of the Golden Flower* represents one of the most radical of these spirit-based methods. Virtually the whole text is devoted to the subtleties of this simple practice of reversal or turning the light around.

There are numerous Chan, Zen, and Taoist sources containing descriptions of tips and techniques for inducing, exercising, and integrating the experience of the golden flower blossoming. The fundamental premise and practice are suggested in the plainest terms in the teachings of Dahui (Ta-hui), a famous Chan Buddhist master of the twelfth century: "Good and bad come from your own mind. But what do you call your own mind, apart from your actions and thoughts? Where does your own mind come from? If you really know where your own mind comes from, boundless obstacles caused by your own actions will be cleared all at once. After that, all sorts of extraordinary possibilities will come to you without your seeking them."

There are also many Chan stories for initiating the golden flower exercise. Some of them are very simple, but they can be used over and over again.

A student asked a teacher, "What is Buddha?"
The teacher said, "This mind is Buddha."

A student asked a teacher, "What should one do when arising and vanishing (of thoughts) goes on unceasingly?"
The teacher said, "Tsk! Whose arising and vanishing is it?"

Once a teacher asked a student, "Where are you from?"
The student said he was from such and such a place.
The teacher asked, "Do you think of that place?"
The student said that he often thought of it.
The teacher said, "The thinker is the mind, what is thought of is the environment. In the environment are mountains, rivers, land, buildings, people, animals, and so on. Now turn your thought around to think of the thinking mind; are there so many things there?"

These Chan structures illustrate some of the ways that attention can be arranged to induce the golden flower experience. It may be possible to apply this use of mind to psychotherapeutic theory and practice by means of its transcendental understanding of the self, its method of experiencing the self beyond the quirks of personality, and its concentration on the elemental source of autonomy and self-mastery.

To the therapist, the golden flower teaching offers techniques of developing deeper insight and greater awareness of human potential, as well as a means of contacting patients at a level of mind that is not affected by psychic afflictions. To the patient, it offers an independent means of self-knowledge beyond the domain of conditioned personality, judgment, and opinion.

Properly used, in the context of contemporary life and not as an exotic, half-understood cult, the practice of golden flower meditation certainly has the power to dispel the influence of neurotic compulsion. Rightly understood and correctly practiced, it does not have the dangers Jung attributed to it because it does not submit to the fascination of what he referred to as unconscious contents of mind.

The exercise of turning the light around is in fact so penetrating an avenue to insight and transcendence that it is tempting to consider applying its theory and practice to the search for direction in treatment of some of the more serious disorders currently being addressed by the psychiatric community, crippling conditions such as those now known as acute manic depression, schizophrenia, psychosis, and multiple personality disorder.

It must be kept in mind, however, that it would be completely foreign to the teaching and spirit of Buddhism and Taoism to suggest that any idea or practice can be regarded as a cure for all ills, or that any spiritual exercise can automatically bring about the desired regeneration regardless of the mentality and attitude of the practitioner.

In the traditional psychology of ancient Buddhist and Taoist schools, psychoactive exercises like the golden flower were part of comprehensive programs, not magic wands all-powerful in themselves.

To say that greenery needs light, earth, air, and water does not diminish the importance of any of these elements; but it may be necessary to emphasize the importance of one or another when it is missing or insufficient.

For ancient methods of mental development to be naturalized in the West, they themselves will have to be in working order to be able to respond and adapt to local needs; and there will have to be ways of expressing and addressing those needs effectively in the context of the new cultures. This is why clinical and descriptive psychology have become avenues for the exploration of formerly esoteric knowledge relating to the nature of experience.

To consider the question of how the golden flower method could shed light on clues to the understanding and treatment of mood and personality disorders, it is useful to work with the Chan concept of host and guest, a simple concept corresponding to the Taoist distinction between the original spirit and the conscious spirit.

From the point of view of the host, or original spirit, everything concerned with mood and personality is in the domain of the guest. But through the process of social conditioning, the average individual comes to be centered in the guest and therefore regards it as the self. As a result the true host is concealed, and it cannot bring out its more objective and encompassing perspective on matters of mood and personality.

When the guest has taken over center stage and the host is no longer in sight, the "switching" that takes place within an individual in response to psychological and environmental factors is taking place from one mood or personality to another; it does not return all the way to the source. The individual can then no longer command the capacity to switch deliberately from a subjective mood or subpersonality to an objective and impersonal state of observant mind.

Thus alienated from the primal source or "host" of the original spirit, the ego seeks integration by attempting to establish order among "guests," the conditioned facades of psyche and personality. Under these conditions, if there develop great disparities among moods or subpersonalities in the absence of ability to "return to the light" of the original mind, then dysfunction and breakdown may result when the strain of attempting to maintain relative order overstresses the natural resilience of the faculty of mind playing the part of the receptionist or answering service for the host. Although the host must be there, it is now hidden and does not respond directly.

Considered in this light, the ability to experience the pure self of the original mind and the capacity to return to it at will can be of fundamental significance in the psychic life of the individual. Even as the conditioned mind goes from state to state in the course of changing circumstances, the golden flower technique provides a means of searching out the host behind the scenes to gain direct input from its creative energy and inspiration.

This host, or original spirit, can occasionally be glimpsed in the space between temporal shifts of mood or personality, but it generally takes practice to stabilize it and use it deliberately. The result of this "crystallization" is a boundless source of potential. If applied with knowledge and without obsession, the method of the golden flower can be of use not only to the psychotherapist, but to the ordinary individual as well; because mind is the pivot of all acts and events, its illuminating effects touch on every facet of life.

There is a great deal of knowledge relating to the use of golden flower consciousness in the teachings of Buddhists and Taoists. These teachings were constructed to assist in orientation of mental exercises, and they need to be understood in terms of their own structure in order to work according to their own design.

In this sense, the need for adaptation does not mean that essential patterns can be distorted. Orientation is as important as the exercise itself, for disoriented meditation does more harm than good.

Seen in this light, traditional Buddhist and Taoist materials on this subject are not propaganda to inculcate religious belief but blueprints of mental functions drawn to provide direction in the understanding and application of psychoactive exercises.

For application of the golden flower mind-awakening method, one of the most useful instructional devices in Chan Buddhist teaching explains the "two minds" in terms of "four relations between host and guest." To focus them in the mind all at once, these four relations are expressed in mnemonic phrases: the guest within the guest; the host within the guest; the guest within the host; the host within the host.

The guest within the guest is the state of the ordinary mind going from one mood, state, or subpersonality to another, alienated from conscious contact with the host behind the scenes.

The host within the guest is the first stage of turning the light around, when contact with the original mind is established even as the individual is passing through shifting moods and personalities.

The guest within the host is a more mature level of attainment, at which the individual can enjoy free access to thought and its products, including ideas, moods, and personalities, without being deceived by them or bound to them.

The host within the host is the original spirit itself, the primal source of consciousness in which is found the hidden "turning point" on which psychic liberty hinges. In one sense, conscious experience of the host within the host follows realization of the host within the guest; yet in a deeper sense the host within the host is not only at the pinnacle but even at the basis of the total experience of golden flower practice.

There are also certain stories from Chan and Taoist tradition that are used to orient and sensitize the mind to this "turning point" in such a way that the capacity to "switch minds" is brought within reach of the ordinary consciousness. A few have already been mentioned.

One of the more dramatic examples of such stories is based on a folk tale about a young woman who was betrothed to a man she didn't love. She ran away to live with her true lover, but eventually died. When her man returned to their hometown after her death, he found that in the experience of the people there she had been at home all the while, having taken to her sickbed shortly after her betrothal.

In modern terms, the parallel with emotional division between outer and inner life is obvious; but can we ask, without assumptions, which one was the phantom?

A Chan master said, "The girl had split souls; which was the real one?"

If we say she was really at home, yet she lived with her lover; if we say she was with her lover, yet she was lying abed at home.

The Chan answer is that both conditions, both "selves," were guests of a formless host.

Another master said, "If you can awaken to the real one herein, you will know that leaving one state of being and entering another is like staying at an inn." In psychological terms, this would suggest that the individual who realizes the true host can enter and exit thoughts, feelings, moods, and personalities at will, being centered in the primal spirit and thus not subject to control by the contents of conditioned states of consciousness.

One of the great advantages of using such stories to jog the mind is that the very act of remembering the possibility of "switching" already places psychological distance between host and guest, thus dispelling to some degree the mesmeric influence of thoughts, feelings, moods, and personalities.

A parallel story from Taoist tradition is the famous butterfly dream of the sage Chuang-tzu. In this classic tale, the philosopher relates that he dreamed he was a butterfly, having a wonderful time fluttering about from flower to flower on the zephyrs of spring.

On awakening from this pleasant reverie, however, he found that he was no longer sure whether he was a man who had dreamed he was a butterfly, or whether he was a butterfly now dreaming he was a man.

The issue of this story is not its superficial question of which psychic contents to identify as the self but is in the act of recalling attention to the "turning point" revealed in between states, the formless "opening" or "aperture" through which the real self of the formless host can be seen and experienced in its own purity and freedom.

By this means it is possible to detach from conditioned states and identities without thereby becoming dissociated from the realm of ordinary experience. Thus the individual can always resort to renewal from the very source of creativity.

This is what Taoists call returning to the "root of heaven and earth," from which extradimensional vantage point it is possible to experience higher enlightenment right in the midst of the mundane world.

If this can be accomplished in reality, there is no reason why psychic events such as extreme mood swings or personality changes should assume control of individuals to the extent of becoming crippling handicaps. Even if this practice is understood in theory alone, it can still offer a perspective on human psychology that will allow for an objective and nonjudgmental approach to the understanding and treatment of mood and personality extremism.

Jung's reasons for warning people away from golden flower practice were ostensibly based on what he perceived as cultural incompatibility. It was his belief that

Europeans of his time lacked the proper psychological basis for the yogic practices of Chinese, Indian, and Tibetan religions. Therefore Jung thought it only reasonable that Westerners should not imitate Eastern methods; and he underscored his point with a proverbial Buddhist warning about incorrect use of practices.

Jung quarrelled not with the method of the golden flower, but with the Western attitude toward technology of any kind. His remarks on the Western mentality suggest avenues of study, but he does not examine the cultic behaviors that make imitation methods ineffective. Had he done so, Jung could have found that neither the reality nor the imitations of spiritual practices are limited to East or West.

Furthermore, Jung does not show how his method is actually equivalent to the golden flower practice. Apart from the fact that he was faced with a garbled translation of a corrupt text with the last few chapters missing, Jung was admittedly preoccupied with expounding his own theories.

Jung's concern with the problems of cultural differences led him to believe that the golden flower practice developed from Chinese tradition, in spite of the fact that he had evidence of its existence in Western tradition. Jung apparently misunderstood descriptions of the exercise partly because of Wilhelm's mistranslation and his own lack of experience.

To deal fully with Jung's treatment of the golden flower teaching would lead us afield from the point of this work, which is to expose the original teaching itself. The purpose of mentioning Jung here is to reopen a door of inquiry by questioning the limits of the limitations he presumed.

Jung's ideas on the golden flower, and their significance in relation to Western thinking about Eastern thought, are more fruitfully treated in the context of his total work on Eastern subjects. Nevertheless, they provide a useful counterpoint to the original tradition when highlighting psychological practicalities of the golden flower exercise.

One reason for this is that Western versions of Eastern mental exercises active during the sixty years that have elapsed since the original publication of *The Secret of the Golden Flower* have been informed in part by Jungian interpretations of Eastern practices.

Among the problems that Westerners have traditionally faced in working with Eastern meditation practices is the fear that mind-stilling exercises will prevent them from thinking thoughts that they need to think. This is also a concern in the East, where there are many warnings in meditation lore to avoid excessive stilling.

There are two main objects to stopping thought in Buddhist tradition. One is to open up space to clarify thought by distinguishing compulsive habitual thought from deliberate logical thought. The other is to clear room for the conscious operation of nonconceptual insight. Practitioners are carefully warned to avoid becoming intoxicated by the peaceful tranquillity of thought cessation; as the Chan proverb goes, "stagnant water cannot contain the coils of a dragon."

The golden flower practice can stop thought temporarily, but it does not warp reason. It enables one to think deliberately rather than compulsively. This use of mind opens a wider space for thought, with the ability to think and observe thought with detached clarity, so that one can put down useless thoughts and take up useful thoughts by means of independent discernment and will. The speed of its direct perception can also see at a glance where a train of thought will lead, conserving untold mental energy.

With any exercise that stills the mind, at first there is a tendency for random thoughts and images to occur with seemingly greater-than-ordinary frequency and strength. Jung became aware of this phenomenon and attempted to exploit what he thought was its potential as a means for exploring the unconscious. He was also aware of danger in this, and he stresses this danger in his works on both Eastern and Western alchemy.

In golden flower practice this problem is avoided by relinquishing all obsession with thoughts and images that come to mind in the course of the exercise. It is only after the actual awakening or blossoming of the golden flower has taken place that examination of mental phenomena with detached objectivity is considered possible. Before this breakthrough, too much introspection of psychic contents is viewed as a distraction from the primary purpose of arriving at the source of awareness itself.

Golden flower exercise is not focused on forms of images or ideas, and in that sense it is not and cannot be culture bound. For this reason it is not peculiarly Chinese, nor is it known and practiced by Chinese people in general through the influence of their cultural heritage.

To adapt a practice to a new cultural setting is one thing; to turn it into something fundamentally different is another. In order to benefit from whatever is useful in Eastern teachings, they need to be reduced to their essence and allowed to develop in their new environment. What is necessary is the primal psychological seed, not the temporal cultural husk.

Taoist and Buddhist teachings explain that their structures and terminologies are not sacred in themselves, but are means of arranging attention to elicit extra potential in vision, being, and action. Independent perception and autonomous conduct are not general ideals in the Confucian and Hindu societies within which Taoism and Buddhism existed; they are part of a transcendent interior culture that has no national boundaries.

The opening statement of *The Secret of the Golden Flower* includes the provision that people should establish a firm foothold in the ordinary world before they try to cultivate the blossoming of the golden flower. This means that they should be able to function adequately in their own culture and society, whatever that may be. The golden flower practice is not primarily a therapeutic method for severely unbalanced people; it is a way of higher development for ordinary people.

Yet it is also true that some forms of neurosis are built into civilized society itself, and many ordinary people suffering slightly from mild neuroses are well integrated with their everyday world. The reason why the golden flower method is not particularly recommended for severely neurotic people, or for people with schizoid or psychotic tendencies, is that the enhanced receptivity and sensitivity fostered by the practice might exacerbate feelings of illness and fear.

The thoughts and images that compel the neurotic and psychotic could become more overpowering in the early stages of golden flower practice, when the "demons" of thought assail the mind as it relaxes its conscious set in anticipation of the attempted switch-over to nonconceptual awareness. Getting past this stage to experience penetrating insight into the essence and source of awareness itself, not associated with any content at all, would be key to any help the golden flower method could offer the severely unbalanced in finding a way out of their hells.

If people with uncontrollable mental problems do turn to the golden flower method for help, they could be better off with the guidance of therapists who have themselves experienced the original mind of humanity and can calmly view the various realms of thought and perception as so many planets in a vast and endless space. For their part, therapists to the mentally bedeviled need the unattached buoyancy and independent objectivity of penetrating insight, so the golden flower exercise could be useful to them in a very direct way in the investigation of processes of mental illness and liberation.

Works Cited

Chang Po-tuan. *Understanding Reality: A Taoist Alchemical Classic*. Translated by Thomas Cleary. Honolulu: University of Hawaii Press, 1987.

Liu I-ming. *The Inner Teachings of Taoism*. Translated by Thomas Cleary. Boston: Shambhala, 1986.

Liu I-ming. *The Taoist I Ching*. Translated by Thomas Cleary. Boston: Shambhala, 1986.

Liu I-ming. *I Ching Mandalas*. Translated by Thomas Cleary. Boston: Shambhala, 1988.

Liu I-ming. *Awakening to the Tao*. Translated by Thomas Cleary. Boston: Shambhala, 1988.

Immortal Sisters. Translated and edited by Thomas Cleary. Boston: Shambhala, 1989.

Li Daoqun. *The Book of Balance and Harmony*. Translated by Thomas Cleary. San Francisco: North Point Press, 1989.

Zen Essence. Translated and edited by Thomas Cleary. Boston: Shambhala, 1989.

The Secret of the Golden Flower: A Chinese Book of Life. Translated and explained by Richard Wilhelm, with a commentary by C. G. Jung. Translated from the German by Cary F. Baynes. San Diego: Harcourt Brace Jovanovich, 1961.

Jung, Carl G. *Psychology and the East*. Translated by R. F. C. Hull. Princeton, NJ: Princeton University Press, 1978.